Dear Jicca +
Remember
to invest in
you!
Blessings!
Deaunder
10/19/04

Everything Has a Price!

Library of Congress Card Catalog No.: 98-941-96
ISBN # 1-892096-00-5

Cover Design: *D. Kent Ross*
Cover Concept: *The Ishai Creative Group, Inc.*
Page Design & Typography: *Lisa Fraiser*
Author's Cover Photo: *Robert Sargeant, CPP*
Author's Photo: *Rafael Tongol*
Author's Cover Photo Make-Up: *Katherine Carey*

PRINTED IN THE UNITED STATES OF AMERICA

EVERYTHING HAS A PRICE!

---

*If you have the strength to survive,
you have the power to succeed!*

VERAUNDA I. JACKSON

Acknowledgements

*In all thy ways acknowledge Him
and He shall direct your path!*
— *Proverbs 3:6*

I am extremely thankful to my creator for his inspiration and the constant reminder that without Him I am nothing, but with Him *all* things are possible!

Mom and Dad, thank you for loving me. You always taught me that I could be whatever I wanted. I am especially grateful for my strong foundation of faith, which was instilled in me at an early age. Thank you Rose and Donald for allowing me to be a part of your lives. To my Grandma Vera and my entire family, thank you for all of your love and support.

A very special thank you to my best friend, Jaydee, for your constant friendship and unconditional love. Thank you for believing in me and encouraging me to follow my dreams. When the waters were rough, you continued to sail with me!

Thank you to my faithful spotters, Ruth Witherspoon, Robin May, Rebbeca H. Miller, Patrice Walker, Sandra Smiley, Brenda Hiesey, Vernon Bryant, Dashonya Wyche, Denise Jones, Veronica Valdez, and

Helen Heim for always being there to help me lift life's weights.

This project wouldn't have been possible without the late night reading of my editors. Thank you for your honesty, your comments and your willingness to work with me on *Everything Has A Price!* Special thanks to Rebbeca H. Miller, Denise Jones, Sandra Smiley, Jaydee Aiwohi, Ruth Witherspoon, and Deborah Austin, Ph.D.

To my Delta sorors, thank you for embracing me into a wonderful sisterhood.

Finally, thank you to The Ishai Creative Group, Inc.: Ricc, Lorenzo, & Richard for believing in me and making my vision a reality!

I wish to express my sincere gratitude to all of the people who have shared words of support, encouragement and expressed faith in me.

Chapter One

The Opening Statement

This book is dedicated to all of those people who have tried and thought they failed. Life is about hurdles...the key is to keep jumping. You only fail if you stop trying. Each time you jump another hurdle, you accomplish something. You move further along in the race. Have you ever just taken a moment at the end of a hurdle to reflect on how far you have come, not to mention how many hurdles you jumped successfully? Well, I took that time not to long ago. I was amazed by what I saw.

I was asked to speak for Delta Sigma Theta's scholarship award ceremony one spring. I was honored by the invitation. However, I was troubled by the analysis the committee used to select me. My sorority sister called me on the phone to inform me I was selected to be the keynote speaker for the Minerva awards. She proceeded to tell me I was chosen because I was a young prosecuting attorney and a college professor. I was a "success." I was someone who could inspire the young people.

Interesting! When people looked at me, what they saw was someone who was "successful." My opening statement of the speech expressed my thoughts on the matter:

A wise man once said that success is a journey, not a destination. Many people see me as a black, twenty-eight *year old Assistant State Attorney and an Adjunct Professor. People appear to be impressed by my credentials. When I look in the mirror, I see something very different...I see that God is a great and a merciful God. He has brought me a mighty long way. I see a person who spent nineteen years in school, a person who studied diligently. I see a person who is paying over $70,000 in student loan debt to be where she is today. When I look in the mirror, I see a person who was, and is, willing to pay the price. Young people...Nothing is free! Everything has a Price. The question I want to ask you is simple: Are you willing to pay the price for your success?*

The standing ovation at the end of my presentation brought tears to my eyes. Members of the audience approached me asking why hadn't I published my story. Truthfully, I wasn't sure. There were several speaking engagements that followed. Each time, I was approached about motivating others to be willing to pay the price. Finally, I sat down at the computer and said a prayer. The result is this book.

I can not express in words the strength that overcomes me each time I look back. I realize having the strength to survive is what gives me the power to succeed. I also realize that EVERYTHING in my life has had a cost. The question has been how much was I WILLING TO PAY FOR IT!

I have chosen to share some of my hurdles with the hope that they will inspire you to pursue your happiness. I encourage you to reevaluate where you are on your journey. Are you measuring your success by material wealth or social status? I challenge you to find yourself in each chapter. Finally, I invite you apply the lesson in each chapter to your own life. Believe it or not, the same strength you depend on for survival gives you the power to succeed!

CHAPTER TWO

DON'T GET CAUGHT UP!

I once heard a defendant in one of my cases say that he had caught another charge. My ears honed in on his conversation with the inmate sitting next to him in the courtroom. The man went on to say how he knew he was going to catch a charge as soon as he saw the deputy. I could not help thinking, "This man just does not get it!" You catch a ball. You catch a cold or the flu. But you don't catch criminal charges. He had been accused of selling drugs. You don't catch drugs; they don't just fall into your lap. You get them from someone and sell them to someone else. The key is that YOU have to take some action for the drugs to be in your possession and for them to be sold. Where he was caught was in the mentality that it was not his fault. He was under the impression that the "system" had him in court, not his own actions. It was as if he had no choice in the matter. He was here because he got caught up.

It is so easy to get caught up in so many things: life, a man or a woman, a job, money, or children. Anything can catch you if you are not in control of your own life. I have had so many occasions where I got caught up. The funny thing is that you don't even realize it is happening. It is like you wake up one day and ask yourself, "How did I get in this situation? Why didn't I see it coming?" Then the guilt starts and you say, "I am smarter than this. I can't

3

believe I let this situation get this far." The sad part is that often getting uncaught is the hardest part. Kind of like gaining weight. You wake up and you see you have gained ten pounds without realizing it. But boy, taking that ten pounds off can take a lot of sweat and hard work. Putting on the weight was not hard at all.

John Parker was one of my firsts in many ways. I met John when I was fifteen years old. His brother was a basketball coach at my junior high school. I danced on a drill team that performed at the basketball games. John says that is where he first saw me and he just knew he had to have me. In fact, his words many years later were that I "presented a challenge for him." My best friend at the time was Alison. Alison was the coach's daughter and John's niece. Alison introduced me to John after a game and for the next three and a half years I would be caught up.

John was a 6'3" tall basketball player and football player at a rival high school. I did not like John very much at first. He was big compared to me at 5'2" tall. He was arrogant and spoiled, to say the least. On our first date...my first date, we went to a park. We walked around and talked for a while. I had on some white jeans and this little red, white and blue sailor top. John was intrigued by the fact that I had nylon knee-highs on, with some nice low heels. So what did he do? He ripped them. I thought, "What an immature jerk!" He laughed. I thought, "This will be the first and last date with you." He dropped me off at home and I was relieved that this big clown had gotten me home without ripping anything else.

It is funny, how with a few phone calls my mind changed. I think it started out with my just saying, "I'll talk to him to get him out of my hair." But at some point, he said I love you and I said it back. Before you know it, I was caught up in love. Don't get me wrong, for fifteen I was not doing badly at all. Love was a lot worse for some of my friends. Compared to them, I was doing real well.

John had a red Camero and a job, which meant he had some money. John was good to me. He took me to the movies, out to eat...mostly pizza and hamburger places, but at fifteen, that was cool. John's mother, Mrs. Parker, was always kind to me. His brother, the coach, was cool despite being my teacher the year before. I liked being around John and I liked being around his family. I talked about him all the time. I talked to him all the time. I wrote about him in my diary. I thought about him all the time. I was definitely caught up in him.

I was kind of popular in school. I was in speech and debate, the drill team, Flag Corp, student government and lots of other extracurricular clubs. I was also smart, as defined by standardized tests and report cards. I had been in private schools most of my elementary years. I started public school in junior high. I met John when I was in the ninth grade. I felt somewhat settled in the public school environment by the time I started dating John. I was an honor roll student (for the most part) in advanced classes. But I was not prepared for someone like John.

He was the total opposite of me. I guess that is what attracted me to him. I liked the fact that he was an athlete. I liked the fact that he was a big guy. (I haven't dated anyone under 6'0" tall since I met him. I feel like I have my own personal bodyguard if the guy is big.) I even liked the fact that John was a "bad boy." Not a goody-two-shoes like me. I had been called an Oreo: white on the inside, black on the outside. I had been called a nerd because I did well in school. I had been told that I talked "proper," which in my neighborhood meant I talked like white folks. I was told that I thought I was cute because of my light brown eyes and shoulder length hair. John made me a regular black girl. With him, I could just hang out and be me.

John had a different lifestyle than I had. He drank beer. I had never tasted beer before I met him. He was not a virgin by a long shot, but I was. He was the youngest of four kids. I was the oldest of two. My father was a preacher and my mother worked for the police department. His mother stayed at home, and his dad worked in a factory. He got a long leash from his parents. I had a very short leash. John intrigued me. It was cool for him to be my boyfriend. I can remember telling my friends that my boyfriend played football at Apopka High School like he was an all-star NFL player. When he gave me his senior class ring I thought I was really special. It was a twelve in men's size. I wore that ring on my size seven finger like it was a huge diamond. I was a sophomore then and my mother and father were separated. Looking back, I think that John became my family. He was a way for me not to think about or deal with what was going on at home.

You can get caught up in one situation because you don't want to deal with another one. In my case, I didn't want to deal with my parents' separation. The more I got into other things, the easier it was to deal, or should I say not deal with my home situation. It was my philosophy that maybe everything would just disappear if I immersed myself in something else. So I worked hard in school, I got involved in extracurricular activities, and I got an after school job. John just topped it all off. He was the one person in my life at the time that could make everything all right, or so I thought.

John would tell me that he loved me. He cared about what I was doing. He was my support group. John was not dedicated to his education. As a matter of fact, I helped him his senior year with his homework. My mom worked a second job at night in a local department store because we needed the money. I would meet John sometime after Flag Corp practice and I would do his homework. I normally did mine at school or on the city bus, so doing his was my way of repaying him for all that he was doing for me. I could not see it at the time, but I wasn't doing him any favors. I was really cheating him. He was cheating himself. The school system was cheating him. He was caught up in being a great athlete, being cool, and getting the girls. The school was promoting him because he was a great athlete. He did not realize he would have to pay a price for not being disciplined in school, for having someone else do his homework and for playing with these girls.

That's what I mean when I say it is so easy to get caught up! You don't see it coming. People or circumstances will make you feel like you are on top of the world. The thing they don't tell you is that those people or circumstances control that world! It took me a while to learn this lesson with John. I was a virgin when I met him and planned on staying that way until I got married. John's niece, Alison, had a friend by the name of Anna. I knew Anna because we all went to junior high school together. We all lived within three or four blocks of each other. But in high school, Alison and I stayed together while Anna was bussed to a different school. Anna changed my life as well as John's. I was caught up in John, but he got CAUGHT by Anna.

Anna was a shapely girl. She had more curves than I did, and I guess more sex than me. I say this because for the first year and a half that I was with John, I refused to have sex with him. I would always tell him that I did not want to get pregnant. I wanted to go to college. The next phrase out of my mouth was, "If you love me then you will wait until I am ready." Well, he did not pressure me about it. Instead, he went somewhere else to get it. That somewhere was to Anna. I don't quite remember how I found out about Anna, but I knew. I knew that John would sleep with her on a regular basis. I knew that she was doing things that I would not. And I knew that she wanted him. Things got out of control at some point. I told John that I loved him, but that I would not sleep with him as long as I knew he was sleeping with Anna. Each time, he would lie and say he was not.

It was in my sophomore year that I started getting calls from Anna. She would call my mother's house and tell me she had been with John after school, while I was in practice. Or that John picked her up from school while I was in practice. I would act calm and in control while she was on the phone. But when I hung up, I would be hurt and mad at the same time. I would call John and ask him where he was. I would tell him it was going to be over if I found out he was lying, knowing he was lying the whole time. I did not want it to be over. He was my life at the time. I needed him, no matter what he was doing behind my back. He was good to me when I was with him. I didn't see him with Anna. I never caught them. So maybe she was lying. I would tell her that I was not going to fight over a man. I had too many other things going for me. I would hang up with an attitude. With one little "I love you", John would have me caught up again.

Senior proms are supposed to be fun, especially if they are with your sweetheart. This was when the stuff hit the fan. Anna had been calling me and telling me that John was taking her to his senior prom. I would calmly say, "We will see", and hang up. I bought my dress and he asked my mom if he could take me. My mother laid down the rules and I was on my way to my first prom at fifteen. As we left the house, Anna was standing across the street in the cul-de-sac with a knife. I thought, "This girl has lost her mind. She is caught up in someone who does not want her and she is making herself look like a fool." I got in the car, John said something to her and we were on our way to the Hilton at Lake Buena Vista. I had a great time dancing with John and his friends. I was home on time and went to bed that night thinking, "John loves me. He proved it tonight by going to his senior prom with ME. He showed Anna who he wanted to be with, ME!" Little did I know, they were still sleeping together on a regular basis. This foolishness continued for the next year while I stayed caught up in schoolwork, extracurricular activities and, don't forget, love.

I was a grade ahead, so at sixteen, I was a junior in high school. Things were going crazy all around me. My parents were officially split. My brother was living with my dad, I was living with my mother, John was still sneaking around with Anna, and I was trying to bounce it all off of me. I could not control what was going on at home so I decided to put all I had into my relationship with John. I decided that I was old enough to make a decision. I decided that if I had sex with John, he would stop having sex with Anna. He would be all mine. My life would be stable. Believe me when I say that you can be more caught up in someone or something than you ever knew was possible. Having sex with John did it for me.

I won't go into the details because they are private to me. But I will say that John swept me off my feet. He was a true gentleman and teacher. He made it really special by telling me that he wanted to marry me, and I believed him. I guess I was lucky because he represented love as I knew it at the time. It was a good experience for me. I loved him even more because of it. The problem was that he did not stop seeing Anna. I was under the misconception that the reason he was sleeping with Anna was because men his age needed sex, and if I didn't give it to him, he would get it somewhere else. Thus, my decision to give it to him. What I know now is that he would have been sleeping with Anna no matter what I did because he could get away with it. He knew he was my first, he knew I was in love, he knew that I was caught up! He cheated on me because I allowed him to!

My senior year was a traumatic one. I needed John more than I ever had. I moved out of my mother's house at the beginning of my senior year. I went to live in the

Young Women's Christian Association (YWCA) downtown. This was a neat place for me to live. There were two dorms. One was for 16 to 25 year olds. The other for ages 25 and over. We had a pool, a recreational room, a cook and a cafeteria. There were usually two girls to a room. Rent was around $40 per week. You could work off half of your rent by keeping the grounds, working in the kitchen or at the front desk a couple of days per week. I did this and kept my rent quite affordable. I worked at a Fanny Farmer Candy store in the mall to pay the balance. I would catch the city bus to school and to my job after school. John made it his business to pick me up if I worked past dark. This made me feel good, not to mention safe.

The women at the YWCA were from all walks of life, but most were different from me. The rules at the YWCA were simple: you had to work or be in school, no children allowed and no men in the rooms. I lived by all of them. Many of the older women had relocated to Orlando or had suffered some type of abuse in their lives. Most of the younger girls were kicked out of their homes and had no place else to go. I had chosen to leave my home because I didn't want to deal with my parents' divorce and my thinking I was grown didn't help. I got to be an adult at the YWCA, with some supervision. I went to school, I went to work, and I saw John when I wanted. It was a wonderful life until September of that year.

I had only been at the YWCA for a couple of months. I had to walk about six blocks to the central bus terminal to catch the earliest bus to school. I usually walked with one or two other girls but this particular morning, Patricia, my regular walking buddy, was sick and was not going to school. When I left the YWCA it was dark. I would walk over a block to Orange Avenue where it was pretty well lit and haul butt to the terminal. Patricia and I had seen a white truck for the past few days.

The driver was a middle-aged white man, probably in his early thirties. Each morning he would yell something out to us and we would ignore him on some days and yell back on others. Well, this morning I was by myself and decided the safest thing to do was to ignore him.

I walked about a block without seeing him and was sighing a breath of relief when suddenly he came walking around a corner and grabbed me. He pulled me around the back of a building with my mouth covered. I freaked! I couldn't scream at first. I could not fight him...all I could do was pray, "God, please don't let this man kill me!"

I tried to remain calm and think. If I could just think, maybe I could stay alive. My brain would not think. In looking back, I think your mind has a screen saver. It blanks out things that may be detrimental to you. I can't remember all that happened. I do know I was thrown to the ground in a gravel parking lot behind a business. I know that the man pulled up my skirt and pushed my panties over and entered me. It seemed like forever and then he left. I know I was called a nigger, and all I could do was cry. I opened my mouth to scream, but nothing came out. I could feel my back being scratched by the rocks underneath me. I thought about the feeling of the rocks on my back instead of the man being inside me. After he left, I just screamed and screamed and screamed with tears running down my eyes.

I somehow made it back to the YWCA. I took a shower to clean that shit off of me and out of me. I got in my bed. I held my stomach. With the tears still flowing, I asked God for one thing: "Please don't let me be pregnant from that white man!" I knew at that moment that if I was, I would abort it. I would go to John and I would tell him. I knew he would believe me. I knew he would give me the money, and I knew he would go to the abortion clinic with me. But I did not want to have to do any of that. I did not want to go through anymore. I just wanted to forget it ever happened!

I tried not to think about what happened, but it would creep into my mind without warning. I wanted John more than ever now. I wanted to be with him every minute that I could, because when I was with him I did not have to worry about anybody hurting me. He would take care of me. He would protect me. He was my life. I remember him asking me on several occasions what was wrong. I would just say nothing and secretly pray that my period would come in a few days. I would not let him touch my back or take off my clothes. He knew something was going on, but I refused to tell anyone if I could help it. This was my secret and I was going to deal with it.

I tried to go back to school, but I couldn't unless someone was walking with me. Even with Patricia right next to me, I always felt that man was somewhere nearby, watching, waiting. I changed the way we walked to the bus station so that I would not have to pass the building where I was violated. I felt that this man had taken something from me just months after I had made the decision to give myself to the man that I loved. He took something from me when I was just learning about being intimate. But he took a lot more than he will ever know! I started skipping school on a regular basis. I would get dressed in the morning to go to school, walk out the door and get a block or two down the road and then turn around. I stayed in my room at the YWCA all day. I made sure no one saw me. If a counselor caught me skipping school I would get kicked out. My life became a series of situations that turned into lies.

I had a friend who was older at the YWCA. I would get her to write letters for me. The letters would say that my parents were going through a divorce and I needed to go to court or that I was sick. Both of which were true for the most part. My parents were going through a divorce and I was sick. I was sick of thinking about what had happened, I was sick of lying, I was sick of having this awful secret. I just wanted to graduate and go to college. I could start over there.

I cried when I got my cycle that month. I was so thankful that I was not pregnant. All I could say is that God had answered my prayers. It was on this day that I was glad my parents had taught me about prayer. It was this day that I was glad I had read the Bible and knew that God would never leave me or forsake me. He knew I was caught up. The only thing that I could not understand is why He let this happen to me. I was so relieved that I did not have to tell anyone. I could go on with my life now.

I still had a problem in school. I am not sure how I did it, but somehow I managed to keep my grades up while skipping a large number of days. I just could not walk to the bus station by myself. No matter how hard I tried, I just kept seeing that truck and that man. I would get physically sick. I would turn around and go back home. I didn't even tell John that I was skipping. I know he would have made me go to school, even if he had to take me. At the time he was working the night shift at Citrus Central. He had gotten a full time job in the factory that his dad worked in making really good money straight out of high school. He would call me every morning before school to make sure I was up. I would say that I was up and pretend that I was off for school. I would talk about school in the afternoon as if I had been there. When I went to school, I acted as if I had not missed a day. I went on test days and did assignments, but I did not participate in any extracurricular activities. My junior year I had been a peer advisor and helped other teens deal with their problems yet, here I was in a major crisis and I had no one to turn to.

Well, I almost made it through without having to tell anyone. One day, I was called in to the assistant principal's office at school. It was around the last month of school and my graduation check was completed. The assistant principal knew me quite well because of my involvement in so many activities. He looked at me and said that I was in danger of not graduating because of excessive absences. All I could do was look down. My heart sank. I had to tell. I listened to him tell me the school board policy on absences and that he was going to have to call my parents to verify why I had missed so many days of school. Tears started to swell in my eyes. I told him I needed to have a female in the room. We had one female assistant principal. She appeared almost instantly, it seemed. I wanted a few minutes to think about what I was going to say. I did not want to cry. I did not want to say I was raped by a white man in front of a white man. I had dealt with this over the last seven months. I did not want to deal with it again. Stuff just started swirling in my head. Did they have to call my parents? What would they say? I knew I was going to be asked why I had not told anyone. I had no answer for that question. Would I have to talk to a counselor? I did not want to talk to a counselor; I was okay now. I needed John! I needed him right now. I wanted to tell him first. I wanted him to be there with me. I wanted him to make everything okay.

Instead, I had to tell the female assistant principal that I was raped. I had to tell her it was on my way to school and that I just could not make it some days. I told her that I had kept my grades up and begged her to intervene on my behalf. I remember clearly telling her that I did not want to have to tell this story to anyone else. She took my hand and said okay. I am not sure what happened next. All I know is that John picked me up from school that day and I went to his house.

I told John what happened. He was mad. I guess for several reasons. First, I had not told him. Second, he felt helpless. He tried to conceal some of his anger and focused on whether or not I was okay. Through tears I said I was, and that he had helped me through it even though he did not know it. I reminded him of the times when I would not let him touch me, and it seemed to hit him hard. He was at a loss for words. I told him to call my dad and tell him. I couldn't. I knew the school had called my mom, but I didn't know much beyond that. I had no clue what was said or whom my mom had told. But I just did not want to discuss it with anyone other than John.

I am sharing these details so that you can understand that life just happens; that things can just get away from you. Your world can be turned upside down while you watch it happen. I think about that year of my life now and it is as if I was not really there. I was caught up in a man, I was caught up in a real life trauma, and I was caught up in trying to graduate. All of these situations crept up on me without warning. It is strange how you muster up the strength to keep living. For me, I knew I was getting caught up in a whirlwind. It felt like a tornado that was moving me across a field. I was just looking at it all from afar. I really didn't know how to stop it.

Matters got worse when my dad came to pick me up. He brought his wife with him. I really wanted it to be just him and me. I was always a daddy's girl. I really needed it to be just us this one time. I recall standing outside with John and his mother. I kept thinking, "I don't want to go. I don't want to leave John. He is my anchor right now. I need him." There was nothing I could do about it. I had to go with my dad. I got in the car, not sure of what was going to be said. I remember only one part of the conversation. "Rhondie, are you sure you were raped? Because I think you just made this up to cover for you and John having sex." I was devastated! My daddy did not believe me! His wife never said a word. (I don't blame her; I would have been quiet too!) I responded by saying, "If John and I were just having sex, why would I miss school?" My dad then asked me if I had been to the doctor to be tested for diseases and to find out whether I was pregnant. I thought to myself, "See, this is why I didn't want to tell anybody! Because of stupid questions just like this." Hell, no, I had not been to the doctor! That would mean telling them why I was there. That would mean calling my parents. It would mean someone else touching me in places I did not want to be touched. That would mean the police getting involved. Hell, no, I had not been to the doctor! I was smarter than that! Now I was just mad! I told my dad that if I was pregnant I would be way pregnant by now and everybody would know it. So no, I was not pregnant and I was not covering for having sex with John! I was silent the rest of the way to the YWCA.

About a week or so later, I overdosed, or tried to, on some sleeping pills. I got sick to my stomach and the counselors rushed me to the emergency room. I was so overwhelmed by everything that had taken place, I just could not handle it. I was seventeen years old and sinking! My spirit was broken, my soul was robbed, and my heart was hurting. I had got caught up in the worst way. I could not see any way out. So I was going to make one. This was probably not a good idea. I got to the hospital and they made me vomit up all the pills. GROSS! My stomach was really sore then. I was so tired and ready to go home. The doctor made me stay in the psychiatric ward for the night. I guess they watched me while I slept.

The next day, John came to see me. That was exactly what I needed. My mom and dad came and it was decided that I would move back home with my mom for the last few weeks before graduation. I was leaving for Florida State University a couple of weeks later. John and I had gotten engaged over the Christmas holidays and he swore he was going to marry me. Life was suddenly bearable again. I am not sure I really understood, at that time, what death really meant. I am not sure what made me think that ending my life was the answer. In retrospect, I lost control of my life. I lost control of who I was and placed too much value in situations and people.

I graduated with my class that June. John was not there. I was hurt. I did not understand why he wasn't going to come to my graduation. After all, I had skipped school to go to his graduation. I had bought him his favorite cake: coconut. Where was he now? Why wasn't he there for me? My family came, but I missed John. I wanted him to be a part of this special day for me.

There are signs in life that we are getting caught up. The reality is that often we don't want to see those signs. We ignore them. We make up excuses and find reasons to interpret them differently. My signs were very clear, I just chose not to see or read them.

Two weeks later I left for college. I was happy that I was starting a new life. I was also sad that I would be leaving John. He asked me not to go. He asked why I could not go to the University of Central Florida right there in Orlando. Why did I have to go to school away from home? To be truthful, I just wanted to get away. I wanted to start over. For the most part, I did start over.

John and I talked a lot on the phone. He paid the phone bill. He sent me money to come home on a regular basis. College was full of new faces, and new friends. It was a new life, except for John. Sometime in my freshman year, I started to realize that he had been my life for the last three years. I started to wonder what our future would be like. Would Anna be in this picture? I found out quickly.

I was home on a break. The day I was to return to college, I asked John point blank, "When did you see Anna last?" Something within me knew he had seen her recently. Something within me knew something was wrong. I just could not put my finger on it. John looked me in the eye and lied, "I haven't been seeing her." I said, "Okay, but if you are lying I will find out." I did not know my answer was a few hours away. Anna saw John's car at my house and called while he was waiting with me for my ride back to college. Anna called my mother's house and asked to speak to John. I could not believe the nerve of this girl. He was at my house with me and she was calling for him as if he lived there! I gave him the phone and looked as pissed as I could. I don't know what was said, but he hung up the phone, then said he had to go. Go where? I thought, "Not to Anna? What had she said?" I had won this battle many times with her. Where was John going? My heart sank as I said in the strongest voice that I could, "If you walk out of this house, that is it." John looked at me with a troubled look and said he really had to go. He turned and walked out of the door. I slammed the door shut and cried. Within five minutes, Anna called back to tell me she was pregnant with John's baby.

It is at times like these that you must make yourself look at why you are in certain situations. Is it because of happenstance or because you allowed yourself to get caught up? For me, it was totally my situation. Meaning that I had let myself get caught up. All the signs were there for me to see. I chose to ignore them. So when I got the call from Anna, all I could do was say, "I wish you and John the best." I could hear the sound of victory in her voice as she told me that she was a couple of months pregnant. I knew at that moment that I had to make a choice. I had to get uncaught. I told Anna that she could have John. I was not going to help raise her child and I was not going to live with her as a part of my life anymore. The ugly side of me could not resist one final comment, "Anna, that is your life and your child. John is not the one that will have to get up at night with that baby. John is not the one that will have to alter his lifestyle to raise that child. You, on the other hand, will always have to be there. While you are raising your child, I will be in college preparing myself for a better lifestyle. It is a shame that women feel as though having a child is the way to catch a man."

I left to go back to Florida State University within an hour of that conversation. My heart was crushed.

People say that time heals all wounds. That may be true, but deep cuts leave scars. John had scared my heart. I wondered how he could let this happen. I wondered how he could do this to me. I thought that he loved me. I believed that he loved me. Now, I felt like a fool. On the four hour drive back to Tallahassee, I filled my friend Jennifer in on the details of my now ex-boyfriend and his soon-to-be fatherhood. Jennifer, a brilliant eighteen year old, who had competed against me in speech and debate for the past three years, listened intently to me. When I was done, she made one powerful observation, "Veraunda, you knew he was cheating on you all along. Why are you upset now that Anna is pregnant? Does her being pregnant really surprise you? She did not get pregnant on her own. John was a willing participant and so were you. John did what you allowed him to do. You stayed with him despite his cheating on you. You should be glad that this happened. Now you are free to find someone who deserves someone like you."

I realized that John had been caught up just like me. He got caught and now he was going to have to pay the price. The price of child support. The price of being attached to a woman that he claimed he wanted nothing to do with. The price of freedom. He has never been married and still lives with his mother. John has four children now. He pays so much child support that he can't afford to move out or have the luxuries he always wanted. He did not learn from being caught by Anna. So, he keeps getting caught. Each time, it is costing him. John and I are friends now. Over the years we have talked a lot about the mistakes we both made. He is starting to understand the concept of "everything has a price." The true test comes in whether he is willing to pay the price.

Jennifer was a very pale and very skinny white girl. I always thought she acted much older than her age. She had a wisdom about her that I enjoyed. We would ride to and from college together in her pale blue Buick, discussing all kinds of issues. Teenage pregnancy, abortions, welfare and affirmative action were among some of the really heated debates. The catch to these conversations was always the color line. White people did this, black people did that. It was during this trip that we both realized that people, regardless of race, allowed themselves to get caught up in circumstances and situations. Once they were caught up, they could not figure out what to do next or how to get out of the situation. Anna's pregnancy was my way out. This realization did not make the pain go away. However, it did open my eyes to the notion that I had been caught! It made me think about all of the warning signs that I had ignored. As Jennifer put it, "You can't expect to keep running stop signs and not get a ticket. Or worse, get in an accident that may take your life. Veraunda, you are lucky, you just got a ticket. Pay it, and then don't get caught running a stop sign again."

Look for the stop signs instead of ignoring them. Understand why the stop signs are there. Just like in driving, they all serve a purpose. Usually, to protect the driver. Drivers make excuses: "I was running late", "No one is ever at that intersection", "I did look both ways before I ran it." The same excuses can get us killed. Life is no different. There are yield signs, caution lights, and stop signs. They are in our lives to direct us. We must be able to recognize what they mean, but more importantly, we must be willing to let them guide us. We can't get caught up in blaming others for where we end up. We are the drivers. We must determine our destination and what route we want to take to get there. Sometimes, the road is quite a challenge. Don't let delays and detours translate into denial or defeat. The key is not to get caught up in the challenges and circumstances, but to overcome them.

The man in the courtroom that had been accused of

selling drugs intrigued me because he could not see that he was the driver of his destiny. Not the deputy that arrested him. Not me as the prosecutor, or the judge as the sentencer. It was not the system that had him here. None of us had thrown him anything to catch. What he caught as a result of his actions was a prison sentence. That was the price he had to pay for getting caught up. Now the question for him is how many more times is he going to get caught up? Each time he gets caught, just like in life, there will be a higher price to pay.

Apply the lesson in this chapter to your life:

What am I caught up in?

_____

_____

_____

_____

How did I get caught up in this mess?

_____

_____

_____

_____

What can I do to free myself?

_____

_____

_____

_____

What price will I have to pay if I continue to be caught up?

_____

_____

_____

_____

CHAPTER THREE

WHY RIDE THE BUS,
WHEN YOU CAN DRIVE IT?

I have worked since I was fourteen years old. I have had all kinds of jobs. I have been a research assistant, law clerk, library assistant, candy sales clerk, radio personality, television show host, cashier, limo driver and bus driver. Driving a city bus was one of the coolest jobs! For the most part, I have enjoyed all of my jobs. When I don't like them anymore, a door seems to open in a new and better direction. That is exactly how I became a bus driver, or as I like to refer to it...a coach operator.

Shortly after my eighteenth birthday, I interviewed with Taltran. Taltran is the transit system operated by the City of Tallahassee. At eighteen years old, you barely know how to drive a car. In fact, I did not get my first car until I was eighteen and a sophomore in college (I totaled the car three weeks later). I was finishing my first year in college. My current employer was the All-American restaurant...McDonald's. I was a swing shift manager as a seventeen-year-old college freshman. I had been a crew chief at fifteen years old.

McDonald's hired me at fourteen. I worked at several of the Orlando locations. I started out at a small franchise on Orange Avenue and worked my way over to International Drive, one of the highest volume stores in the country (International Drive is the tourist haven in Orlando). At any given time, busloads of people would come into the restaurant. At fifteen, it was a fun challenge to get the people served in record times. I actually liked working at McDonald's. I could tell you how long it took to make a shake, a burger, or fries.

When I started college, I needed a job and quick. So, I went to a sure thing: McDonald's. The store was about four blocks from my apartment. I did not have a car. I walked to and from work on a daily basis. Depending on what time my shift started, I could catch the bus on some days. Riding the city bus was nothing new to me. I rode Tri-County Transit in Orlando from elementary school until high school graduation. I rode the bus to summer school, to after-school activities, and to and from work on a regular basis. I knew a lot of the drivers by name. I knew the routes and stops like the back of my hand.

Tallahassee was a little slower with their transit service than Orlando. This took some getting use to. One day, I got on a bus with this tiny girl driving. She was no more than five feet tall and probably a hundred pounds soaking wet. She was from Orlando. We hit it off instantly. During our conversations, I found out that she lived in the apartments directly behind mine. She was attending Florida A&M University. I was impressed that this tiny girl could handle that big bus. But I was really impressed when she told me that the starting pay was $7.01 an hour. She suggested I stop working at McDonald's for $5 an hour and come over to Taltran. My response was, "Girl, I don't even have a car. How am I going to drive one of these huge busses?" I thought she was joking. I would have never even considered driving a bus. But the dare from her made me want to at least try. The dare was simple: "I dare you to go fill out an application." The next thing I knew, I was catching the bus to an interview with the superintendent of operations.

I can recall thinking to myself, "What am I doing? I don't know anything about driving a bus. All I have done is ride them for years." It hit me at that moment, while I was sitting in the front seat behind the driver, "If I can ride the bus, I can drive it!" At eighteen, I was smart enough to know that you can do anything that you set your mind to. I didn't just want to interview at this point. I wanted to drive the bus!

The superintendent told me that I would have to get a chauffeur's drivers license. I could report for work as soon I as had it in hand. So, at eighteen, I was going to be a coach operator making $7.01 per hour. This was back in 1988 and $7.01 is a lot of money even by today's standards. I was hired as a part-time coach operator. I went back to McDonald's and put in my resignation while bragging that I was going to be a city bus driver. Everyone laughed at me. I laughed, too. It did not sound real. I was in college to become a lawyer. Now, here I was, going to drive a city bus? People say money is the root of all evil. In this case, money was the root of my becoming a bus driver.

I reported for training on the first day wearing with a nice skirt outfit. The skirt was ankle length. My first embarrassing moment came when my supervisor Ralph told me that I probably did not want to wear skirts for this job. Ralph was probably in his early sixties at the time. He was a black man who had retired from the Air Force. Ralph did not play. To prove it, the first day on the job, I was getting behind the wheel of a thirty-foot bus with a skirt and heels on. The advice from Ralph was simple, "Tomorrow, try some pants!"

Working for a transit company was a totally different world. The makeup of the company was very interesting. There were drivers, mechanics, dispatchers, information attendants, and of course administrators. The biggest part of the work force was drivers. Most of the drivers were much older than I; many were forty years plus. At the time, this was a predominately male arena. I don't believe there were more than ten women driving at the time. All of the supervisors were male. All of the administrators, except one, were male. So, here I come, at eighteen years old, in college and saying that I wanted to go to law school some day. People thought I was playing. Many thought I was just a big talker and overly ambitious. But as time went by, actions spoke a lot louder than words.

I started driving on our campus routes that circled Florida State University and Florida A&M University. Students riding the bus thought I was crazy! There were always questions from the students. "Aren't you afraid to drive this big old bus?" "How are you going to stay in school and do this too?" When I drove regular routes, there were questions there also. "Are you the real bus driver?" "When did you start?" "Can I have your phone number?" "Are you married? " (I would always answer yes. I wore John's engagement ring to make sure that it appeared official). People still come up to me today asking, "Didn't you drive the bus in Tallahassee?" I am just as proud today that I was a bus driver as I was then. It was a wonderful opportunity for me to develop many life skills at a very young age.

We worked eight to twelve hours a day. Most of the time, it was at least ten hours. We drove in ninety-degree weather with no air-conditioning on some days and in thirty degree weather with no heat on other days. Most morning runs started between four and six in the morning. The days usually ended between six and seven in the evening. Lunch breaks were an average of twenty minutes. For an eighteen-year-old, this was a big adjustment. I had to be on time every morning, drive a huge block of metal, get people where they needed to be on time and do it safely. This was not McDonald's, where if a customer got a cold sandwich or the wrong order they could just get over it. People were depending on me to get them to work, school, or medical appointments. If I ran late, they ran late.

If I was not paying attention, I could kill someone.

Despite the long days, hot busses, no power steering, and tightly run schedules, I loved my job. I enjoyed driving the bus. I would greet the passengers with a "Good morning", or "How are you today?" I felt like I was on top of the world. I would sit in that driver's seat, thinking, "Look at me, driving this big old thing. Who would have ever thought that me, Veraunda, would be driving a city bus?" I would whip that bus around corners like it was a compact car. I'd hit a curb here or there, but in over four years, I never had a serious accident. I enjoyed the challenge. But more importantly, I think I enjoyed being different. I enjoyed being this young woman doing a job that I was not supposed to be doing.

There were many days that presented a challenge. Within two months of being hired, I was stopped by a Tallahassee Police Officer. At the time, part-time drivers did not have to wear uniforms. I had on some plain clothes and my hair was in a ponytail. The officer asked me if I was really the operator of this bus. I said I was while showing him my employee ID card. The officer, a male by the way, gave me this goofy smile and said in a southern drawl, "Girl, I can't believe you can drive this big old thing." He then asked for my driver's license. When he saw that I was born in 1970, he started laughing. I laughed right along with him. It was funny to me too. I was driving the very bus that I had relied on to get me around for years. Ha ha...and I'm being paid to do it. Ha ha ha...I can ride the bus for free now. Ha ha ha ha, I got the last laugh!

Life is this huge picture. How much you get out of it will depend on how you look at the picture. I looked at driving the bus as one of the best things that had happened to me. I wanted to be Miss Taltran. It did not take me long to get there. I learned how to work as a dispatcher, an information attendant, and a reservationist for our Dial-a-Ride busses that carried the elderly and handicapped.

By the end of my first year, I was not only driving busses, I was dispatching them, giving route information on the phone or at the terminal, selling tickets, and taking reservations from the elderly and handicapped, not to mention doing presentations at local public schools.

Many of my co-workers were not thrilled about my being so diverse in the company. As a matter of fact, many of them labeled me because of it. I really didn't care what they thought. I have been labeled all of my life because of one thing or another. Being labeled can be fun. I find it a challenge. People judge you because of what you do, or where you are in life without having one clue how you got there. I didn't sleep with anyone to do these jobs; I just worked hard. I had to get up every morning like they did. I had to have an open mind and not see myself as only a bus driver. I was willing to try new positions in the company. So, if that made me someone's pet, then, oh well. My mission was to be me, no matter in what position I was. I could drive the bus while engaging in an intelligent conversation with the best of them.

The people who were jealous, I wrote off as people who were really mad because they had no ambition. I just did not see it as my fault or my problem. I was here because I wanted to be here. I was here because I liked my job. I knew that one day I would be moving on to bigger and better things. I was here because it was a stepping stone, just another life experience that would make me who I am today: a strong woman, willing to accept a challenge, and trying to make a difference.

As a bus driver, you see it all. The drunks who always want to sit right behind you, carrying on an incoherent conversation, the business people who are just trying to make it to work on time, the students who are late for class because they overslept, but now they want you to be in a hurry, the young teenage mothers who come out of the house half-dressed, the teenage boys who have more money than you do because they are selling drugs, the elderly who need to go to the grocery store every week because they can't carry more than two bags at a time. As a driver, you don't have the privilege of picking your passengers. You interact with them all on a daily basis whether you like it or not. I now realize that this was the beauty of being a bus driver. You can deal with them all, and if you really care, you can make a difference in a few of their lives.

The only time I remember being scared was on a night run in French Town. French Town was a predominately black area; a high crime area according to the police. I had never had any trouble on this run. To me, all runs were about the same. But this one night, a man in his late thirty's got on the bus at the station around eight PM. It was dark. There were only a few passengers on the bus when this man decided, in his drunkenness, that I was a good target for his rage. He started by sitting right behind me. When I was driving, we had quite a few busses where there were no plastic or metal dividers between the drivers and the passengers. The next thing I knew, he is talking about how he hates women. I was only nineteen years old. I could have cared less about his hatred of women. So, I ignored him. That made him mad. He yanked my hair to get my attention. I had no formal training on bus etiquette when dealing with hostile passengers, so I did what I knew from growing up in a black neighborhood. I acted hard. "You have got one more time to touch me, and you will be walking home! I am not going to tolerate this foolishness from you, Mister! Now you either shut up, or get off!" This was funny to him, so he yanked my hair again. I wanted to turn around and backslap him, like the old folks did when you were told not to interrupt a conversation between grown people. I slammed on my brakes, turned around in my seat and yelled, "That is it!" I got on the radio to call the night mechanics. I told them to send the police right away. They asked me what was wrong. I said, "I got a drunk that is touching me." (This way, the police would hopefully hurry to my rescue.)

In the meantime, I was going to act hard while praying that God would not let anything happen to me. There were a couple of other people on the bus, but they were not saying a word. So much for community involvement or protection. I could hear them groaning about getting home late, but no help was going to come from them. I took the attitude that if they weren't going to help me, then they would get there when I got them there. TOO BAD! (I'm still not sure what I wanted the passengers to do.)

The police came within a few minutes. I was glad to see them because, while I was waiting on them, the gentleman was saying, "Okay, I am sorry. Don't put me off." The next minute, he was calling me a bitch. The police escorted him off the bus and I continued on the route about ten minutes behind.

I saw the man a week later. He came over to my bus apologizing for his actions the week before. I accepted the apology. I explained to him that I just don't have time for foolishness. I am working, trying to put myself through college and he gets on the bus pulling on my hair and acting stupid. He hung his head while saying he was sorry again. I told him he needed to be sorry, he had made other people late. I was still acting hard. As far as I knew, he could be on my bus on any given day. I wanted to be sure he knew I was not scared of him, nor would I put up with any crap from him. I never had another problem out of him, despite seeing him off and on over the next three years. I felt good when I saw him throughout the years because I had shown him that I was no wimp of a woman driver. I could hang with the best of them. I had won his respect.

People watch you. I had very few problems as

a driver. My guess is that people knew I was serious. As a matter of fact, many of my friends today still tease me about being a mean bus driver. I don't think it was mean, I prefer to call it...strict. No eating, no drinking, no loud talking or playing on the bus. This was a serious job. I was serious about it...most of the time. I am a firm believer that people do what you allow them to do to you. I was only going to ask once, the next time there was going to be some action taken. Usually being asked to get off the bus. On the other hand, a warm smile and a kind good morning worked just as well as the serious face the majority of the time.

The passengers on a bus represent every category of people you will meet in a lifetime. They have different attitudes, philosophies and backgrounds. I have talked to different people about any subject you can imagine while driving the bus. The most interesting thing is that I could discuss the same subject with ten different passengers and learn something new from each one of them. When you drive for ten to twelve hours a day, believe me, talking becomes a lifesaver! But more importantly, that bus becomes a tool to a whole new world.

I thought about anything and everything when I drove the bus. You have plenty of time to think as a bus driver. I daydreamed about what my life was going to be like in ten years. I thought about day-to-day problems. I wondered about why things existed, how they were created, what made someone want to create them. But I was really intrigued by the people on the bus. I would play games to try to guess what they did for a living, whether they were married, if they had kids, what kind of home they lived in and, last but not least, why they were riding the bus.

Take me for example. I had ridden the bus because I was in college with no money to buy a car. When I finally got a car, I wrecked it and was stuck on the bus again. However, I wasn't going to be a bus rider forever.

I knew I was going to save up some money to buy myself a car. For me, the bus was a temporary method of transportation. Some passengers had physical disabilities that prevented them from driving. Another set of passengers were financially challenged. This means that they did not have the money to buy a car. I always wondered about this group of passengers. Would they ever buy a car? How long would it take for them to get the car? What kind of car would they buy? A new car that cost more, or an older car that is cheaper? If they got a used car, they could be driving sooner. There were elderly passengers that chose not to drive any longer. They just did not feel comfortable behind the wheel anymore. Some passengers just did not want to be bothered with the traffic. Why should they pay a car note, maintenance, and gas when the bus was a convenient, as well as a cost-effective way to travel to and from their destinations? Last but not least, there were the no-ambition passengers. The passengers who could drive if they wanted to, but they didn't. The passengers who complained about the bus system constantly. If they wanted to be off the bus they could. But these passengers were content with riding and complaining. I hated these riders!

Let me tell you, driving the bus is better than riding the bus on any day! The first major advantage is that you get your own seat. As a passenger, you have to share with whoever decides they want to sit next to you. If the bus is really crowded, you may even have to stand during your trip. The other big advantage is that as the driver, you control the climate on the bus. As a passenger, I'd always be too cold or too hot. I could ask the driver to adjust the temperature; but the driver made the ultimate decision.

Life mirrors the bus ride in many ways. You can choose to ride as a passenger, or you can take control of your life as the driver. But YOU have to make the decision. Driving the bus is not an easy job. You have to remember all the different runs, look for the stops, collect the fare, give transfers, answer route questions, and listen for the bell to signal for the next stop, in addition to the hustle and bustle of maintaining a schedule while putting safety first. Driving the bus itself is the easy part. It is all of the other things that come along during the day that cause you to slow down or frustrate you.

Have you ever noticed that there are no rear windows on city busses? I always wondered why this was the case. There are two big side mirrors and a big rear view mirror. The front windshield is usually the width of the bus. But no rear window. After a few weeks of driving the bus, I realized that you should always be looking ahead and to the sides of the bus. This allows the driver to see what is going on around him. You can see what stops are coming up while keeping your attention on the traffic. As a bus driver, you don't need to worry about what is going on behind you unless you are backing up. In most cases, the bus should be heading forward or progressing on a route. Backing up is very rare in a transit bus. In fact, we don't even back the busses into a parking space. The parking lot is even set up so that you pull the bus forward in a space. The bus is parked in a position for the next driver to pull straight out the next morning.

Backing up is very dangerous in a bus. Life is no different. So many people spend time going over territory they have already covered. They dwell on what has happened to them in the past instead of looking at what is ahead of them. This is where people need to decide whether or not they are going to be the driver of their destiny or just a passenger. If you are going to be a driver, part of the job is determining which route to take and what turns to make, while tending to the needs of the passengers on the bus at the same time.

Who are the passengers on your bus? In everyday life, the passengers may be your coworkers who are negative, your family that requires your attention as soon as you walk in the door, or friends who have a crisis they want you to help them through. But, if you are the driver, you must keep your eyes on the road at all times. You can take quick glances at the passengers to make sure they are not out of control. But your priority is driving that bus to its destination while trying to balance all of the other duties that come with being a driver. You can't allow a passenger to distract you and cause you to miss a turn or have an accident. There have been so many times that a passenger thought I was listening to them when I was really watching the road. It is not that I did not care to hear what that passenger was saying, but I had to drive the bus. That was my job; everything and everyone came second to that responsibility. I could not choose who was going to ride my bus, but I could keep them from interfering with my job.

There were times when I had to put people off of my bus. In each case, the passenger was interfering with my ability to do my job. I could not tolerate such behavior. I was the driver; I had to drive. If a passenger was keeping me from doing that by any type of behavior, then they were putting my life in danger as well as the other passengers. In defensive driving, bus drivers are taught to always protect your box. This is the square that you are sitting in. You are taught that if you are involved in an accident, try to keep the driver's box from getting hit. The reason is that you are likely to be seriously injured or killed if struck in that square. The rest of the bus can survive a crash with much less damage. This makes sense if you think about it. The seats for the passengers are raised above the wheel level. The passenger seats have handles to hold onto. As the driver, you have no cushion to save you. This is why you are taught to protect your box.

If you take this "protect-your-box" attitude as the driver of your destiny, you could save yourself from a lot of injuries. Don't get me wrong, as the driver, you are always concerned about the safety and well being of the passengers. However, if you are not taking care of yourself, how can you take care of the passengers? If people are distracting you, then maybe you need to put them off the bus. In some cases, a warning may be sufficient. But your priority has to be getting from one point to the next, safely and on time. If you are arguing with passengers, or allowing them to distract you, that is an unnecessary delay. Being the driver of your destiny means being in control of when you stop, when you go, and how fast or slow you want to go. This should be your decision, not the passengers. If you are the driver, you know how your bus works. You know how well it takes turns, what amount of strength you need to make a tight turn around a corner, or how much pressure to apply to the brakes. You have driven this bus day after day. You know how it works. A passenger on your bus, in most cases, doesn't have any idea about how your bus works. All they know is that the bus is supposed to come at a certain time, it costs a certain fare, and it should get them where they want to go. As the driver, it is your job to educate your passengers as to how YOU will drive YOUR BUS.

That is why being a passenger is not always the best position. As a passenger, you are depending on someone else to get you where you want to go when you want to be there. This means you have to leave early, wait outside in the sunshine or rain, pay a fare, get a transfer, switch busses, and then ring the bell for your stop. This, of course, is assuming that you know where you want to go. If you are not sure, then you are depending on the driver of the bus to give you directions or tell you when you are at the right stop. You can only get on or off the bus if the driver stops and opens the door for you. What if the driver misses your stop? Then you have to get off at the next one and walk back. What if the driver is late? Then you are going to be late, too. It may mean having to wait at the bus station fifteen to forty-five minutes for the next connecting route. Everything depends on the driver if you are the passenger.

Perhaps you can't be the driver at this moment. That is all right. After all, there are age restrictions, physicals, and other qualifying requirements that must be met before you can drive a transit vehicle. So your goal while you are a passenger is to prepare yourself to become a driver. Maybe you are a secretary in your office. There is no reason why you can't set your goals early on to become an office manager in the company. Why settle for office manager when you can run the company or start your own? We all have to start out riding the bus. As a passenger, you should not feel bad that you don't have your own car yet. Riding the bus can open a lot of doors for you. You can learn the routes as a passenger, get to know the drivers, and most importantly, map out your destination. That is what I have tried to do all of my working years. I learn as much as I can as an employee. I know that knowledge is power. I can use skills that I learned while working as a cashier at McDonald's over fifteen years ago in my profession as a lawyer and an educator. McDonald's was a foundation. Each job that I have had since that time were layers on my journey. It is how you look at life that will determine your ability to succeed.

If you are not in a position to drive the bus, you can always make the trip smoother as a passenger. You can get to the bus stop early. I always hated when people were running late, then wanted me to rush to get them where they had to go. Catch the bus that is going to get you to your destination a few minutes early instead of right on the dot. If something happens, you can still make it to your destination on time, despite driver delays. Don't rely on the driver to remember where you want to get off. You ring the bell! You control your destination. The bell signals to the driver that one of the passengers is ready to get off the bus. So many passengers assume that the driver knows them well enough to know where they want to get off. This is false! People change stops. Just because a passenger gets off at a certain stop most of the time does not mean that they want to get off at that stop this time. Passengers also assume that someone else is getting off at their stop, so they wait until the last minute to ring the bell. Don't depend on other passengers for your destination. You ring the bell when you want to get off the bus.

How does this translate into the real world? Simple. Your boss, your spouse, your friends, or your children need you to ring a bell when you are at a stop. Your supervisor cannot guess when you need a vacation, or have personal problems or a heavy workload. You need to ring the bell to tell them that you need help, want to get off the bus here, or transfer to another run. Your family members will not be able to tell that you are dealing with a difficult supervisor who is making your blood pressure sky high unless you ring the bell. They may know, as bus drivers know, that you need to get off the bus at some time, but they don't know when. They are waiting on you to signal that this is your stop.

The cool thing about life is that you can make it what you want it to be. One day while I was driving the bus, I saw a stretch limousine. The chauffeur had on a tuxedo and the passengers were all dressed up. I thought, "Hey, I want to do that! That looks like fun." I wanted to be a limousine chauffeur. Why couldn't I be? I was a bus driver, wasn't I? I was sure that the limos had power steering and air conditioning. The bus was much longer and bigger. The next thing you know, I was looking in the yellow pages under limousine services. Tallahassee only had a few companies listed. I called each and every one of them. Only one was interested in hiring a new driver...Class Act Limousines. I spoke with a man named Isaac who invited me for an interview. I was excited! I was writing down the directions when I realized the company was in French Town. This was the area that had the reputation for being a predominately black, crime-infested community. "So what," I thought, "I want to drive a limousine!" I was in for a big surprise! I arrived for the interview and the building was a funeral parlor! I almost died! (No pun intended!) I sat in my car for a minute to gather myself. I saw the black Cadillac limousines in the parking lot. They were nice. But two of the three were funeral limousines! I crossed my fingers that I was not going to be driving the hearse!

Isaac was an older black gentleman. I liked Isaac from the first moment we met. He had a huge smile on his face as he reached out to shake my hand in the foyer of the funeral home. I introduced myself. I am sure that my face had a look of absolute fear on it as we walked to his office. I did not want to see a dead body in a coffin. Lucky for me, the coffins were on the left side of the building and we were going to the right. I was enlightened in one of the strangest interviews of my life. It turns out that the funeral home owners were all professional businessmen who wanted to expand this business to include limousine transportation. Most funerals were during the day on Saturdays. The cars were expensive and sat in the lot the majority of the week. So, why not rent them out as limos for special occasions to make some money? I breathed a sigh of relief when I heard this. Isaac had done some driving for the limousine company, but he was really the funeral home director. He needed someone who could work nights as a driver. I was his girl. He was excited because I had my chauffeur's license, not to mention experience. We went for a test drive while discussing the terms of employment.

I would be making $6.00 per hour plus tips.

Clients must pay 15% gratuity up front. The car rented for $30-$45 per hour. Boy, was I cheap labor, I thought. I would work nights as needed. I could wear a black pants suit and a tie if I liked. The company did not have money to buy me a tuxedo. (I was a little disappointed because the chauffeur I saw had a tux. It was a sharp look in my opinion.) The catch? I would drive for funerals on occasion at a straight $7.00 per hour. I worked at Taltran on most Saturdays, so I thought, "How bad could this be?"

I did well with Class Act. I made extra money while driving for proms, anniversaries and a few funerals. Class Act was a starting place for me in the limousine industry. I attended a concert and met New Edition and Al B Sure within the first month of driving. Unlike driving a bus, as a chauffeur you spend most of your time sitting. Tallahassee was no more than thirty minutes from one end to the other, even with traffic. Most clients would eat dinner prior to their engagement. I would sit in the car, studying for school. Easy money, if you asked me. I liked driving the limo. Everybody would look at you, wondering who was in the back.

The only part I did not like was the funerals. I helped Isaac out from time to time. I would answer the phones at the funeral home or drive for a funeral. This was hard for me because I was such a cheerful and happy person. I loved to smile. You don't smile when you go pick up a family who is about to lay their loved one to rest. In fact, I often would find myself tearing up because the family was crying. I will cry with you in a heartbeat. I hate to cry! It makes me feel so vulnerable! I gained strength at the funeral home. I could look at a dead body and not cringe on the inside. I would hold family members' hands or give them a hug while they were greeting well wishers during viewings. You develop a hard shell to protect you from all of the human emotions. But that is all it is...a shell that covers your inner most emotions.

I became bold. I would go with Isaac into the room where he embalmed the bodies. Trust me when I say, one word will describe it...MORBID! The room is always cold and smells of chemicals, mostly formaldehyde. I never understood how I could stand there and not pass out. I can tell you one thing, I don't watch horror movies anymore! The most vivid memory I have of working with Isaac was seeing an infant prepared for a funeral. It was a tiny baby girl who had died shortly after birth. Isaac had wrapped her in towels soaked with embalming fluid. I was curious when I saw the small bundle of towels. Isaac was working on an older man, so I decided to see what was in the bundle. I opened the bundle with apprehension. My heart was beating so fast, I knew this would be the time I would faint. I knew there was a child inside because Isaac had told me there was. But I wanted to see this child. I was accustomed to older people dying, not babies. When I unwrapped the last towel I burst out in a whaling cry. "Oh my God, she is so precious! God, why did you take her?" Isaac grabbed me and walked me quickly out of the room. I asked through tears, "Isaac, how could you work on that baby?" He responded, "Sweetie, this is my job. No one said it was always easy." Isaac told me to take the rest of the day off. At eighteen, the realization of death had hit me dead in the face! Nothing is promised...absolutely nothing! That day, I decided I no longer wanted to work for Class Act.

I was the only black, female chauffeur for miles around and that made it great for me. I had made a commercial for Class Act that was showing in the Tallahassee area. It was about this time that a new limousine service moved to town. VeeVee and Tony Lockhart relocated their south Georgia limousine service to Tallahassee. They had two new Lincoln limousines full of amenities. There was a wet bar, color television, VCR, mood lighting, a partition, and separate radio and cassette players for the driver and passengers. I was impressed. VeeVee was the first woman chauffeur I had ever seen. Not only did she have a tuxedo, she had colorful bow ties and accessories to match. What class! The name of the company was Tally Ho Limos! Cute, huh? Within a couple of weeks I was on the phone. My interview was at their home. The company was a family owned business that was looking for someone reliable to join the team. I was their woman.

Again, we went on a test drive while working out the details of employment. This was a good move for me. They bought the tuxedo and I bought the accessories. I got $7.00 per hour plus gratuity charged up front. The cars rented for $50.00 per hour. I felt good about working for Tony and VeeVee. They were good southern people who welcomed me into their family immediately. Even the dog came along for the test drive. Business with Class Act was off and on. Tally Ho was the opposite; we were always busy. The cars were the newest in town, so they sold themselves. Add Tony and VeeVee's charm...the business was a sure thing. I got some great jobs with Tony and VeeVee.

One of my jobs was driving to a town named Gretna. This little country town is about thirty minutes outside of Tallahassee. I was going to pick up a wedding couple after the ceremony. I got to the church in plenty of time; the problem was parking. The church was one of those old, wooden, picture-book churches that sat right off a two-lane highway. There were cars parked all down the side of the two-lane road. There was no place for me to park the limo. Most of the weddings that I had driven for had an area blocked off or reserved for the limo. Not this one! I went down the country road for about two miles looking for a place to turn around. I could not find one, so I decided to do a three-point turn (I remember this term from drivers education in high school) in the middle of the street. After all, there was no traffic because everybody in this town was probably at the wedding. I did all right on the first part of the three points. The problem came on the second part...backing up. Remember, I said this was an old town? Well, the sides of the roads looked like solid grass. They weren't solid at all. There was a ditch on one side of the road that had grass at least four feet tall in it, which made it blend in with the rest of the roadside. I started backing slowly. Good thing I was going so slowly because I felt the back end of the limo go down. My heart skipped about ten beats.

I was afraid to get out. I did not want to see what had happened. I was really afraid that I was going to have to call Tony or VeeVee to tell them that I had damaged their nice, new limousine. I opened the door, got out with my heels sinking in that country dry sand , and walked to the back of the car. The ditch was really visible from this angle and so was the rear tire hanging over the ditch. There was no way that car was going anywhere. I could not believe this was happening on one of my first jobs with Tally Ho! I walked up to an old wooden home with a screen porch on the front. An elderly black woman greeted me at the door with, "Honey, that's some kind of outfit you have on! You must be running a tad bit late for that wedding down yonder at the church." She had a huge, warm smile that I think only southerners can round up. I politely said, "No ma'am. I am driving that limousine stuck over there in that ditch. Can I use your phone to call my boss?" The whole time I was praying that she had a phone...this house had been there for many, many years, by the look of it. My prayers were answered and she invited me in to use the phone.

I dialed the business number on the old, rotary phone. The rotary phone was killing me. Each time I dialed a number, I had to wait until the little round thing swirled back around. My heart was beating so hard that I thought I might go into cardiac arrest at any moment. I just knew I was going to be fired! Finally, VeeVee answered the phone with her little chipper greeting. The dreaded story came out of my mouth with tears swelling in my eyes. I must have apologized about thirty times in two minutes. VeeVee had three kids and it came across on the phone. "Veraunda, it is okay, honey. Just relax. We will bring you the other car and Tony will wait with that one. We have to use a special towing company because of the long axle in the limousine, but don't you worry. Tony will be there in a few minutes." I was in shock. I was expecting some yelling, some questions, and then the firing. None of that happened. In fact, the last words from VeeVee were, "Aren't you glad you left so early? You never know what will happen."

Well she was absolutely right about that! Tony came within a short period of time. The old lady served me something to drink while I was waiting. My guess is that she was in her seventies. She had never seen a limousine in real life before. She asked me if she could just peek inside. I told her sure and out we went to look at the limousine in the ditch. It made her day. She grinned from ear to ear. "I can't imagine ridin' in nothin' as fancy as this here car 'til I die," she said. I replied, "Ma'am, don't say that. You can ride in one for any occasion." The age and poverty showed in her face as she proclaimed, "Sweetie, this here car probably cost more than that ole shack I live in. Hell, it's almost as big as my house." She chuckled to herself as I pondered what to say next. Older people can read faces. She read mine. "Baby, don't feel bad. I am happy to see you youngins doing so well. In my day, you woodna seen no black man, much less woman, drivin' no car like this here. You so young and probably in college up there in Tallahassee, ain't ya?" I answered with a proper, "Yes, Ma'am." She asked which college. I responded with, "Florida State University." She shook her head from side to side.

43

"See, that's what I mean. In my day, you didn't think about going to no college...now, here you is at the white college. Ain't that somethin'?"

It was at that point that my ancestry flashed through my eyes. This little, sleepy, country town had all the makings of a good old southern, segregated community. I looked around and thought about the roads I had taken to get here. There were no white people on this side of town. No fancy cars or big houses. My ancestors had probably driven nice cars just like me...as chauffeurs...but not for the wages I was making. Certainly not for the tips I was making. Many of them would have never owned a car as fancy as this Lincoln I was driving. That, of course, was assuming they owned a car at all. I had never thought about my driving the bus or limousine in terms of a testimony to people about what could be done if you set your mind to it.

This lady had worked manual labor in fields and in homes to make her living. The pride in this woman beamed from her face. She was proud that I was doing a job that could not have been done by someone looking like me just a few years before. She was proud that I was going to that white college where she would not have been able to go if she wanted to. She made me feel a new sense of pride. But more importantly, she made me want to just keep breaking the mold of tradition and stereotypes. We talked until Tony came with the other car. As I left to go back down to the church, I gave her a big hug while whispering in her ear, "You helped pave the way for me to be going to that white college and driving this big fancy car. You have been such a blessing to me today!" With that kind smile, she whispered back, "No, you have been a blessing to me!"

I drove off down the street with a new friend in Gretna, Florida. I also drove off with a renewal of spirit. I could do and be anything that I wanted! I thought about the fact that I started off riding a city bus to get from place to place. Who knew that I would drive one to pay my way through college? Who knew that driving a bus would land me a job as a chauffeur of a fancy stretch limousine? That's the point. You don't know! I went on to drive the likes of Lou Rawls, Billy Joel, and several other stars while with Tally Ho Limousines.

Each job led to a bigger or better one. I did not have to settle for anything. Case in point? About four years later, I was in law school when Rosa Parks, the mother of the Civil Rights Movement, came to speak at my school. I met her after the speech. She is now a frail, soft-spoken woman in a wheelchair most of the time. I imagined her being tired, getting on that city bus after a hard day's work. I imagined her taking the first seat she got to and sitting down. I then imagined the bus driver, at that time a white man, telling her she could not sit there; coloreds belonged in the back of the bus. I imagined her standing up to him and then being arrested for just trying to sit in the front seat of a bus. People went to jail for the opportunity to sit where they wanted on a bus. Now, here I was some twenty years later sitting in the driver's seat of one of those busses! Why not? If I could ride a bus, I sure as hell could drive one!

Apply the Lesson in this chapter to your life:

Where am I going?

_____

_____

_____

Am I on the right bus? (Am I headed in the right direction?)

_____

_____

_____

Am I a passenger or a driver?

_____

_____

_____

If I am a passenger...what type of passenger am I?

_____

_____

_____

Do I know when to ring the bell?

_____

_____

_____

Am I in the right seat as a passenger or a driver for my current situation?

_____

_____

_____

_____

Everything Has A Price

CHAPTER FOUR

JOURNEY TO JUSTICE

I have heard the saying "Success is a journey, not a destination" many times. When I was younger, I wondered what that really meant. Now that I am older, I understand completely. Everything in life is a journey. Nothing happens overnight. No success is obtained overnight. There is a preparation period whether you know it or not. I, for one, did not really realize that I was being prepared for a career as a lawyer, educator or public speaker. However, the road to becoming all of these things has been quite a journey.

I have attended both private and public schools. I started off in private, moved to public, back to private, and ended up graduating from a public school. By 7th grade, I was attending the public school system on a full time basis. Each school had something to offer. However, my preference was public schools. I think I really grew in the Orange County Public School System.

My first real memory of how different public schools were starts in the seventh grade. In private schools, I wore a dress every day. The dress was below my knees and always had sleeves. At Westridge Jr. High, girls had on mini skirts, sleeveless blouses, and shorts. The whole school system was a shock to me the first year. Kids cursed, did not dress up for school, talked back to their teachers, and ate junk food for lunch. Hey, a kid could get used to this lifestyle! But not me...I was a goody-two-shoes, according to my peers. I dressed nicely, sat in the front of the classroom, did my homework, and made good grades. Not to mention that I was in Advanced Placement classes, which automatically made me an Oreo in my neighborhood. According to the kids in Richmond Estates, an all-black, middle class neighborhood, I talked white, I acted white, and I thought I was white. WHATEVER! This was my first real lesson in racism, as I know it.

Racism for me, in junior high, was the black kids picking at me because I was applying myself in school. Today, it seems absurd. But it still rings true for many adults that I know. Jealousy is a terrible thing. I was a grade ahead of myself. At twelve years old in the seventh grade, how do you deal with such cruelty because you are doing what you are supposed to be doing? I took a novel approach. I ignored it and decided that the better I did, the more that I excelled, I would show the world that it could pay off. I have been on a quest since the seventh grade to prove that hard work pays off. It is strange that here I am, seventeen years later, still trying to prove that point.

One teacher stood out that year. Mrs. Rebecca Height Miller was my AP English teacher. I hated her! She had this southern drawl, big, pretty blue eyes that saw every move you made, and the most agitating thing about her was the constant pushing for me to do better. The nerve of this little, petite white woman from Tennessee telling me that I could do better. I was an honor roll student in AP classes. I was smart and I knew I was smart.

I can remember the layout of the class perfectly. There were rows of desks that faced her desk and her blue and gold Westridge podium. I sat to her far right in about the third seat back. There were only two blacks in our class, so my take on Mrs. Miller was that she was a racist! Truth be told, at twelve I did not know a whole bunch about racists or racism, but it sounded good at the time. I did know however, that there were white people that did not like black people, and vice versa.

I had always gotten away with murder in school. I would get good grades with little effort. Not in Mrs. Miller's class. She actually wanted me to work. Not just do the work, but think about what I was doing and how I was doing it. She would make me rewrite papers. Every time I thought I had a good paper it would be returned with a note saying I could do better. Mrs. Miller's class frustrated me. At the end of the semester, I would have a B on my report card. You talk about a seventh-grader who had problems! Well, the last semester of the year I finally got an A in English. It was about time! After a year, Mrs. Miller, had grown on me. Those big blue eyes, her warm smile and, I must admit, her interest in me, made me wonder why she had been so hard on me. I asked her near the end of school that year. She responded by saying, "Veraunda, you are a smart girl. You have a lot of potential. All you need to do is apply yourself. You were settling in my class. I pushed you because I knew you could do better." Then, with that smile that only Mrs. Miller can round up from the mountains of Tennessee, she said, "I was right, wasn't I?"

Have you ever felt like someone didn't like you? After a while, you realize that the person was really taking care of you the entire time that you were resisting their help. Let me tell you, from that moment on I have admired Mrs. Miller. I admire her because I was just one of many students over thirty years that she had the courage, or should I say energy, to push forward despite the students pushing back against her. She had the ability to see what I could not see in myself: not only that I had potential, but also the potential to be great. She also knew what I did not: that the road would not be an easy one. She knew that I was going to have to find the inner strength to push myself and not settle in life.

Mrs. Miller approached me one afternoon with the suggestion that I participate in the Optimist Original Oratory contest. "The what?" I thought. I agreed after learning what oratory was. (A speech.) Mrs. Miller agreed to be my coach, and at thirteen years old I started my performance as an orator. The Optimist Club held this speech contest every year. The winner of the local contest would go to a district competition, then regional, etc. My first year, my first speech contest, I placed second. Mrs. Miller and my parents were there as I received this nice silver medallion around my neck. I was surprised that I had placed second. Many of the competitors had been competing for years. This was just the beginning for me, literally!

I was involved in many extra curricular activities. I was in the Flag Corp, drill team, chorus, student government, and on the newspaper editorial staff. I twirled flags during football games, danced during basketball games, sang at all kinds of school functions, not to mention working at McDonald's about twenty hours a week. But this public speaking thing had a nice challenge involved. Normally, I was the only minority at the competitions. Where was the challenge? Going into a room with judges who may doubt your ability before you even open your mouth. My goal was to go in and win! I wanted to prove that I could beat the odds. (Of course, I still don't know if the odds were in my favor or not. I just assumed they were against me because of my skin color.) I don't say this in a mean way. I say it because in my world, I was black. I lived in a black neighborhood and I went to black churches. When it came to school, I was in advanced classes with white students. I always felt that I HAD to prove myself. You learn this from the comments that you hear from your black classmates and your white classmates. It is always about proving that you are just as good, if not better than your counter part. For me, it was expected from my white classmates. But it always hurt when my black classmates would tease me for excelling in school.

The oratorical competitions gave me the opportunity to show both groups that I was indeed a winner. In the chorus or drill team, everybody works as a team to put on the show. In speech competitions, it is a one-woman show. I would practice until I could not stand it anymore. I would stand facing my dresser performing my speeches for hours. Every time I messed up, or if I made a face or choked up while practicing the speech, I would make myself start over. The second year that I went back to compete in the Optimist competition, I won first place. Don't tell me that you can't do whatever you set your mind to do!

People have always told me that I talked too much. I would respond by saying, "I'll be talking my way to the bank one day!" The Optimist competition led to my joining the Oak Ridge High School speech and debate team. I competed in only one area: original oratory. Coach Kyker picked up where Mrs. Miller left off. I stayed active in the Flag Corp and other student organizations, but my heart was in the speech team. Once again, I was the only black on the team. By the time I got to high school, I had become accustomed to going to competitions and seeing no one that looked like me. It was a reality that I soon learned did not make a difference in who I was or what I could do.

I won competitions left and right. I would always place, normally in the top three speakers. My junior year, I kicked some butt with a persuasive speech about drunk driving. I placed first in the state of Florida. After a trip to Washington D.C., I was in the top twenty percent of the nation's orators. I was a proud black woman. Why? Because despite my color, I had won! This may sound funny to many of you. For me, it was a breaking of barriers. A victory of the heart, mind, and spirit! It was the revelation that I could do it! I have felt this same victorious spirit on many occasions since 1985 when I placed at the National Oratory Competition. Each time I accomplish something that many people think I will never achieve, I get that feeling of, "I did it!" In spite of everything, I did it!

In the face of these victories, I also get a humbling of my spirit. The humbling comes from the effort it takes to do it! The effort it takes to win. The persevering when you are tired. The victory is special because of the price that it costs to win. That was what Mrs. Miller knew when I was in the seventh grade that I didn't. Everything has a price! The question that only I could answer was whether I would pay it!

After the rape in my senior year, I did not participate in many extracurricular activities. I did not like going to school anymore. I did not like catching the bus when it was dark. I had hit a low spiritually. I did not feel like competing. I had been beaten emotionally in addition to being raped physically. Being raped was what I got for making the effort to go to school. I did not have the inner strength to push myself as Mrs. Miller had tried to teach me. Less involvement became better for me emotionally. Part of me just did not care anymore. I was settling.

In the summer of 1987, I headed off to Florida State University. College was my wake-up call. The alarm had to sound more than once during my college years. I was excited about a new start, a new environment, and new people. My freshman year, I lived it up! I met new friends and ate junk food almost everyday. I even tried out for, and made, the Flag Corp of the Marching Chiefs (The Florida State band). After a few weeks on campus, I had to get a job, which meant quitting the Flag Corp because I could not make the practices.

I still stayed involved with other organizations, like student government. I was a little sister to the Alpha Phi Alpha Fraternity. I went to the campus parties and was having a great time. My biology class had over one thousand people in it. It was held in Ruby Diamond Auditorium, a massive theater hall with a stage that the instructor would lecture from. Yeah right! I was supposed to learn biology with over a thousand other people? Well, my grade proved that I did not get it. I got a D.

I did all right in the majority of my classes, but math and science gave me hell! I brushed those classes off and worked in the classes that I enjoyed. At the end of my first year of college, I had about a C average. College is where I probably needed a Mrs. Miller. Most professors did not take attendance. They could care less whether you showed up for class. As one of my professors said so eloquently, "This is college! We don't babysit! We don't hold your hand! This is YOUR money and YOUR education! Now, what you get for your money is up to YOU!" Most professors did not know your name by the end of a semester. Florida State University had over 23,000 students. If you did not make your mark, you became a part of the crowd.

I was not accustomed to being a part of the crowd. So, in my own way, I tried to make my mark. I fell back on my oratorical skills. In Greek organizations, you are always given a line name. This is a name that says something about who you are. It may be a reference to your personality, physical characteristics, or perhaps a strength or a weakness. My line name was Miss Oratorical. In less than a year, I had showcased the strength of my speaking skills.

I was having a great time at FSU during my first year. I had a sense of belonging. I was doing okay in my classes...not excelling like I was capable of doing, but I was making it. I had a job and my bills were paid (barely, of course). Life was good for me, but by the end of the fall semester of my freshman year, things would change. I would have to realize that I was not trying to make it to a destination. I was on a journey with quite a few roadblocks.

I lived off campus in my own one-bedroom apartment. It was very cheap, with the standard plaid wood furnishings. I tried living in a dorm, but dorm life was not for me. There is no such thing as the end of the day in the dorms. People are up, no matter what time it is. Music is always playing, pizzas are always arriving, and a card game is a sure thing somewhere in the hall. The army should recruit in college dorms because most students do more at night than they will do in a week for a class. When the sun goes down, the campus comes alive. I did not leave the dorm before ten PM to go to a party. The parties would end at two AM. The next stop would be for Krispy Kreme donuts or to a Denny's for breakfast. I did not drink alcohol so I did not have to worry about hangovers the next morning or passing out somewhere. But I started noticing that I was always tired.

I'll be the first to admit that I stayed up really late, but the tired I was feeling should not have been happening to an eighteen year old college sophomore. Tallahassee, Florida is a very hilly town. The campus was a full workout from one end to the other. This was good exercise after eating the pizzas and hamburgers each night. FSU has a beautiful campus. There are red brick buildings and red Georgia clay can be seen as soil for the azaleas blooming the majority of the year. The hills top off the southern charm for the campus. I loved to walk the campus. I thought it was beautiful. I started to notice that I was becoming short of breath after walking short distances. I felt my lungs hurting when I walked up a hill. I could not stay awake for long periods of time without a nap. I had gained about fifteen pounds during my first year of college. But the extra weight should not have caused this type of exhaustion.

The Thaggard Student Health Center was the bearer of bad news my first winter in Tallahassee. I had tested positive for TB. Tuberculosis is not something that I knew anything about. However, the series of tests that I had to take made me aware that it could be serious. The doctor at the health center sent me for chest x-rays at a local hospital. The doctor met with me shortly after the x-rays. I was having trouble comprehending what he was saying. In medical terms, he told me that my chest x-ray had been negative but that my skin test was positive for TB. I was put on some medication that I would be on for a few months. The doctor could not tell me how I had gotten TB, just that it was contagious.

In the next few weeks, I had to make a decision about my classes. I was literally too tired to do anything. I went to my advisor on campus. The recommendation of my advisor devastated me! In light of my physical health, I probably would not be able to satisfactorily pass my classes. Therefore, I should withdraw for the semester. Withdraw? I had just gotten to college! I could not think straight. I started crying. I wanted to know how I would get back in school. What would happen to my financial aid status? What was I supposed to do during this time off from school? The panic hit and my thoughts went wild. I would be behind a semester. People would think I had flunked out of school. I did not want to move back home. I would be the laughing stock of my peers who already could not wait for me to fail.

Mrs. Miller and I stayed in contact after I left junior high school. I called her and told her what was happening. Mrs. Miller has a soothing demeanor. I can't remember her ever getting really mad. She has a sweet, little southern voice that will instantly calm a hysterical child. I have cried on her shoulder more than once. So, I knew that she could help me pull it together. The odd thing about Mrs. Miller is that she does not give advice. Strange, huh? She is a listener who has developed a method of helping people find the answers for themselves. I can't ever recall Mrs.

Miller telling me what to do in sixteen years. That is, other than rewrite a paper!

When it came to your life, she would encourage you to stay strong, keep your head up, and hang in there without telling you how to do it. When you finished the conversation with her, you would know what you had to do to get past the obstacle that was facing you. The cool thing is that the answer was one that was within you. If we are honest, we know what our choices are from the minute we see the hurdle in front of us. We can turn around, we can quit, or we can size up the hurdle and give it our best shot. The hurdle really doesn't care what we do. It is there for those who want to jump it.

Here I was at eighteen with something called TB causing me to withdraw from FSU. I could not and would not quit. I took the medication and rested for several months. I worked just enough to keep the bills paid. I missed the spring semester, but that summer I was back at FSU. I took school a little more seriously this time around. My grades were not as good as they could have been. In fact, I was close to academic probation. My first semester, I had failed math and science, which ruined my grade point average. It was not that I could not do the work. I went to college with the attitude that I had always been a good student. I did not expect the work to be harder in college and it wasn't harder. The problem was my lack of discipline. I did not apply myself. I did not try in many cases. I settled for mediocrity instead of reaching for success. I skipped my eight AM biology class. I would skip my math class. If I didn't feel like doing my work, I didn't do it. I did just enough to get by in the classes that I did not like. No one sent progress reports to my mother. No one harassed me about not doing my best. Most of the people who know you at college really don't have any way to know what you are doing. So, as long as you have a good game face, life appears to be great.

The next major hurdle in my educational journey was just around the corner. I had only been back at FSU for a short time when I found out that I was not going to be eligible for financial aid. I could get some loans, but not enough to cover my expenses. When I met with the financial aid counselor, I was told that I had made too much money while working at Taltran as a coach operator to qualify. At the time, my mother was still claiming me on her taxes. The income from Taltran and her income exceeded the guidelines for financial aid. This was a real joke! I was working to put myself through college. My mother did not have the money to help me. My father and I weren't really speaking during this time, so I had no support from him. I was driving a bus because I needed the money to live, not because it was a glamorous job. The counselor explained that I could apply for independent status and reapply for financial aid the following year. That was great...but what about this year? The counselor suggested that I attend the local community college. Her reasoning was that credit hours were less expensive, the classes were smaller, and I could really work on bringing up my grades.

For the second time in a year I was at a crossroads in my educational journey. The same fears ran through my mind that I had encountered with my first withdrawal process. What are people going to think? I don't want to go back home! I don't want to be a failure! I never considered just quitting. I was out to prove something. The question again was, "Prove what, and to whom?" The detour route over to Tallahassee Community College was a worthwhile trip! Don't confuse worthwhile with easy!

I enrolled at TCC in the summer of 1989. I had about thirty hours to complete to receive my Associates of Arts degree. When I enrolled at TCC, I made up my mind. I was tired of playing around. I did not have a car. I was struggling financially. Time was of the essence. I was going to be serious. I was going to apply myself. I could not come this far and fail. I had the foundation to do well. I had the discipline to do the work. I had potential, but more importantly, I had the potential to be great! I gave myself this wonderful pep talk. I found the inner strength to say to myself, "I am screwing up, but it is not too late to get back on track." Trust me when I say that is a hard thing to say to yourself. But that is the turning point in our lives. That is the place we have to come to in our lives in order to really make some changes.

One summer my mother took my brother and me over to Daytona for an auto race at the speedway. She worked for a bank that was a sponsor for the race. It was a cool thing to watch as a teenager. I watched as the cars zoomed around the track at killer speeds. It bothered me when a car would be in the lead, or close to the lead, then suddenly pull over into the service area. I thought, "Oh, no, just when he was doing so well he has to get a tire changed or refuel." I just knew that the car would never be able to gain his lead back. To my surprise, all of the cars had to pull over at one time or another. The majority of the cars would regain their lead after some hard laps around the track. Of course, as a teenager, I was not looking at life as a journey. I just wanted to see who was going to win the race. The race was exciting because of the pit stops the drivers made. The pit stops created the suspense. Would the drivers be able to get back on the track, focus, and regain their position? TCC was the second pit stop on my educational journey. It was a checking of my engine, changing of my tires, and refueling. I did a complete overhaul!

I took two classes my first summer because that was all I could afford. I had to pay for every class and every book myself. It was my money and I was going to get my money's worth! It becomes a different game when you are paying for everything on your own. You realize that everything really does have a price. You also realize that it is not just how much you are willing to pay, but how much you CAN pay. I did not have a car, so I had to catch the same busses I drove to pay for the classes to get to school. I worked as much as I could at Taltran and the limousine company to make ends meet. I took the math class that I had failed twice at FSU and a humanities class. I got A's in both. My grade point average was a 4.0 for the first semester since high school.

After my second semester at TCC, I was inducted into Phi Theta Kappa, the National Honor Society of two-year colleges. I was racing around the track at full speed now. I gave myself one year from the date I enrolled to complete my AA degree. I had a new sense of direction. But more importantly, I was ready to push myself to the limit. The community college was a different environment. It was the environment that I needed to get back in the race. It was much smaller. Normally, there were no more than thirty students in a class. Not to mention that a full twelve credit hours cost about $300. I had twenty five dollars a week deducted from my Taltran check, which was directly deposited into the Tallahassee Leon Federal Credit Union. At the end of the semester, I would have enough money to pay for the next semester of classes. I would use the tips from the limousine company to pay for my books.

When the summer of 1990 came, I was not only back in the race, I was winning the race! I had renewed my commitment to my education. I was pushing myself and I felt good. The journey was far from over and I knew it. From this point on, I was going to have to stay focused. But more importantly, I was going to have to believe in myself when others didn't.

Prior to leaving FSU, my academic advisor told me that I might want to think about changing my major. I had chosen a major in Communications with a minor in Journalism when I entered college. The College of

Communications was a limited enrollment college. This simply meant that the school accepted a certain amount of students per semester. The selection process was a tough one, based on many things, but one requirement was a minimum grade point average of 3.0. When I withdrew from FSU, I was at a low C average. The advisor said it would be impossible for me to bring my grades up to a B in just four semesters. If I was disobeying my mother, she would talk to us a few times and then she would say, "I can show you better than I can tell you!" This usually meant that she was talked out. The next step would be some physical pain on our butts!

I used my mother's warning as my motto that year at the community college. It worked! I graduated from TCC with over a 3.0. GPA. I showed that advisor that I could do it! Actions had spoken much louder than words. I applied to the College of Communications. A few months later, I received a conditional offer of acceptance. The conditions were that I provide proof of graduation from TCC and that I maintain a 3.0 GPA for the first semester I was in the Communications department. No problem! I was ready to accept the challenge. I had been on this path for a couple of years now in search of my education. I knew the drill. Hurdle in your path? Jump it! If you fall trying to jump it? So what! Get back up, do it again! There is nothing like the feeling of proving you can do it. I was more focused and determined than ever to get my Bachelor's degree in Communications. Next step would be law school!

There was only one question: how was I going to pay for FSU? I went back to the financial aid counselor. I had already started the emancipation paperwork for financial aid. The counselor told me that I would be eligible for student loans, but very few grants. At this point, it really did not matter to me what I had to do to pay for school. The bottom line was that I had to do whatever it took to make it to the finish line. I could worry about repaying the loans when I got my degree. The paperwork was processed. I waited for what seemed like forever, but the letter finally came saying that I was approved for a financial aid package that included student loans. I was officially pulling back on the racetrack after a pit stop!

If you hang in there, you not only stay in the race; you can end up winning it against all odds. My first week back on the campus of Florida State, a miracle happened. Almost every major college has a back to school fan fare. This usually includes a major radio station doing a remote at the bookstore. The radio personality comes out in the station's van. The music is blasting from the speakers. There are free pizzas, hot dogs, wings, and cokes provided by restaurants. Despite the long waits to buy the books, the atmosphere is usually quite festive. The fall semester of 1990 was no different.

I was standing in line like hundreds of other students, eating and joking with friends. After about thirty minutes, I reached the radio personality's table. The gift at this table was a Hot 101.5 Frisbee. Great! Just what I have always wanted! Little did I know that Frisbee would be responsible for my next lap in the race! I asked the disc jockey what he expected me to do with a Frisbee? Surely they had cups or T-shirts instead. Eric Angel was the DJ's name. Eric gave me this big smile and asked me my name. My response was why he wanted to know. I knew how these on-site radio gigs worked. I'd be talking to him like it was just him and me and the next thing you know, I'm on the radio, making a fool out of myself! Nope, I was smarter than that. So I started asking him questions. What the heck; I still had at least another half-hour in line. Eric was a smooth DJ. His voice was deep and sexy. I had listened to him every morning for the past two years. "What's your major?" he asked. I was refusing to cooperate. I responded by saying, "You know, you sound exactly the same as you do on the radio." Again, Eric Angel gave me a big smile. This ping pong type question and answer game went on for a few minutes. Eric ended the game when he said, "You have a beautiful voice. Have you ever considered working in radio?" For some reason, I knew he was serious. This was not a trick. He was not just trying to put me on the radio for a few seconds. He was asking me about a job on the radio.

I know that the grin on my face said that I was flattered, in shock, and of course interested! Eric told me that Hot 101.5 was going to need a part-time DJ on Saturdays. I took his card. A week later I was doing a demo tape for the program director. Don't ask me how, but I walked out of the radio station with a job! What more could a girl ask for? I was starting my junior year at FSU in the College of Communication and I had landed a job as an On-Air Personality! Full speed ahead, I was in it to win it now! There was no way I was going to blow this opportunity!

The first order of business was to find a stage name. I thought long and hard about what kind of name I should have. Most DJ's keep part of their first name and just add something jazzy to it. There was no way I was going to find something to rhyme with Veraunda. So what about Miss V? No. V lady? Lady V? DJ V? It was not happening; the jazz wasn't there. My program director came up with the name "Cindy Spice" a week later. I have no clue what made him put the name Cindy with my personality or me. Now the spice I could work with! If you want my honest opinion, my guess is that he saw it in a XXX movie and liked it! Nevertheless, he was the boss. From then on I would be "Cindy Spice...the original nasty girl!" Trust me, it was not as bad as it sounds.

Cindy Spice was sexy and seductive, yet sophisticated and smooth. It was what she didn't say that made her sexy. I say her because Cindy Spice was my on-air personality. I created her based on my program director's idea. All of us have a little of Cindy Spice in us. I was lucky because I got paid to find her in me for six hours every weekend. I worked the six to midnight shift on Saturdays for the next two years. I loved being Cindy! I loved the perks that came with being a DJ. The pay was not much more than minimum wage, but add in the free concerts, all the latest music, and fame...working in radio was the life. The problem was that it did not pay tuition or rent. So, I juggled being a DJ on Saturdays, driving the city bus during the week, and chauffeuring on the weekends while attending school full time.

Let me tell you, it was not easy but I had a blast doing it. The mere fact that I was working 60-80 hours a week and maintaining a 3.0 grade point average gave me an awesome sense of accomplishment. On average, I slept no more than six hours a night. My body was paying the price, but it was worth every minute that I worked or studied! I had energy like you would not believe. It was a natural high. When you are excited about life, the energy becomes second nature. You make time to study. You find time to rest. It all just comes together.

The two years in the College of Communication were the best! The struggling paid off when I graduated in the summer of 1992 with honors from my major. The price I had paid was nothing compared to the feeling of walking across that platform while hearing my name called as the recipient of the Bachelor of Science Degree in Communication. The price was nothing compared to knowing my family was sitting in the audience watching me become one of the first to earn a bachelor's degree on either side of my family. I had won the race! I started out struggling, but I ended with a victory!

When you have won a race, you know you can run another one. The next race you run may be a longer, more competitive race. The first race teaches you the strategy of racing. You learn how to pace yourself and how to persevere when you really feel like quitting. This was the lesson Mrs. Miller was teaching me in the seventh grade. Don't just race because everybody else is racing. Don't race because someone else wants you to race. Race because it is what you want to do. Become good at racing. Push yourself to reach your full potential and you will always place in the race. I had learned this lesson by my senior year at FSU. I was ready to enter the next race without having officially finished the first one. I wanted to go to law school!

I did not know any lawyers as a child. The first time I met a lawyer was when I was thirteen years old. My parents were getting a divorce. My mother had a female friend who was a lawyer that represented her in the proceedings. The divorce proceeding was a short one. I remember going to the courthouse with my mother and not being given a chance to say much of anything. I remember the judge upset me because it seemed as if he did not care about the case. As a teenager, I honestly did not understand all of the factors involved in a divorce case. But I was smart enough to know that there were two sides to every story. I should have been able to say something. I knew that on television Matlock went to court and everybody had his or her say. I can not say with certainty that my parents getting divorced is what made me want to be a lawyer. However, it made me want to fight for justice.

In January of 1992, I submitted only one application for law school. This was not what the books or counselors recommended. Everything and everyone I had ever talked to suggested that you apply to as many law schools as you could afford and hope that you get accepted to at least one of those schools. I did not have application fees for ten or twenty schools. I did not want to move out of Florida, nor did I want to go to a private law school. There comes a time in the race when you know exactly where you are headed. Something deep inside of you says this is what you should do and you just start that race full speed. The pit crew on the sidelines thinks you are crazy for taking such a risk. But you know that you can win against all the odds. That was the attitude I had about law school. I knew I could get accepted to FSU. I did not have the highest grade point average that I could have, but I had worked hard. I could submit a better package of life experience than someone who had been valedictorian of their class. I had the potential to be a great lawyer; my obstacle was to convince FSU's College of Law!

I will never forget going to the blue U.S. Postal mailbox on FSU's campus with my law school application in a nicely typed 81/2 by 11 manila envelope. I stood at the mailbox with the application in hand and said a small, simple prayer. "Lord if it is Your will for me to go to law school, You will make a way. I am stepping out on my faith that You will give me the desire of my heart. My desire is to attend FSU's law school. Amen." With that simple prayer, I slid the envelope into the mailbox and left my future in God's hands.

There comes a time when you either trust your pit crew or you don't. I trusted my pit crew because experience has proven it more than capable to do the job. That is what I mean by you gain strength from each race you enter. You learn from your mistakes. You start having confidence in your manager and crew based on their performance in each race. There has not been one race that I have lost because I have trusted in my manager...GOD. I have won each race. Winning means different things to different people. My definition of winning is not only finishing the race but learning something each time I race. Sooner or later, if you enter enough races, you will learn how to train for the race. You will learn how to troubleshoot during the race. You learn how to apply mind over matter while focusing on the strategy instead of the situation. This was my approach to law school.

I did not worry about whether I would be accepted after I mailed that application. Instead I developed a strategy for several situations. If I was accepted to law school, I needed to start preparing myself mentally for a tough race. If I was not accepted to law school, I needed to figure out which races to enter that would prepare me to try again later. My alternative plan was graduate school for Communication. I would get my master's degree and reapply to law school. I could keep working to save some money. Both options were positive in my opinion. I had not come this far to quit. I was going for the big win.

It really does not matter when you become the champion, just like it does not matter when you win the lottery. The fact that you won is all that counts. Sure, there are times when we prefer to win over others. However, I don't know one person who will say to the race officials, "You know I really wanted to win this race last year, so just keep the prize now. I no longer want it." The bottom line is if you did not want to win, you would not keep racing.

Four months after applying for law school the letter came in the mail. My heart beat quickly as I said one last prayer. "Lord, whatever Your will is, I will be obedient." This was my way of telling my pit crew and manager that I was going to trust the decision that had been made about my status in the race. I slowly opened the envelope while trying to prepare myself for what was inside. My mind was racing through all the what ifs. Before I knew it, I had pulled out the single sheet of paper. I noticed that my hands were trembling. I forced my eyes to the opening sentence. "We are pleased..." is as far as I got before I started screaming in the street. "I made it! I made it! God, I made it!" For all I knew, the remainder of the letter could have said I was on a waiting list. I did not care. I had won. I was in the big race. After I stopped screaming, I read the rest of the letter, which did in fact say I was admitted for the fall class of 1992. I got the acceptance letter one week before my wedding. It was the best wedding gift I could have asked for! I celebrated by calling everyone I knew that afternoon.

Three months after my wedding, I was being welcomed to FSU's college of Law. I was anxious, excited, and scared. Money was not an issue because I was borrowing money in addition to the scholarships that I had been awarded. I was not going to be living in a luxury apartment, but my bills would be paid. I was starting from the beginning in law school. New people, new administrators, and a whole different way of studying.

In law school, you do one of two things for your grade. You write papers or get a three to four hour final exam. No multiple choice here. It is all essay questions. You get one shot at passing the class. Anything less than a C means you will see that professor the next semester. The first year, your class schedule is chosen for you. All freshman law students have the same classes. The class is divided in half and you pretty much stay in the classes with your half for the first year. My class was a real diverse class. We had doctors who had decided to return to school, nurses, engineers, and students who had their MBA's or Masters degrees. The average age of the students in my class was twenty-eight to thirty-two. Here I was at twenty-two, fresh out of undergraduate school. For the first time in my life, I was intimidated by school. The professors had done an excellent job of explaining that everything is graded on the Bell Curve. In simple terms, this means you are not going to be graded on your work. You are graded on your work compared to everyone else's work. Only so many people can get A's, and only so many people can get B's. The majority of the class will get C's and a few will get D's. How encouraging!

My first semester, I stayed stressed. I studied, which in law school really means read until your eyes deteriorate by at least one prescription. The strange thing is that I enjoyed law school. I enjoyed the reading. I enjoyed the class discussions, which turned into heated debates on some days. I guess I was so happy to be there that my attitude towards law school could be nothing but positive. Did I enjoy taking the four-hour exams at the end of the semester? Of course not! But that was part of the price I had to pay if I wanted to be a lawyer.

I got involved in extra curricular activities. I tried out for and made the mock trial team. This was a team of about twenty-four law students that participated in staged trials all over the country. You prepare like crazy with the hopes of bringing the law school a trophy. I was elected the Chair of the Law School Appropriations Committee my first year and stayed in that position until my senior year. I oversaw the distribution of a budget. I stayed involved with my sorority. I was going to make the best out of this race.

I made law school work for me, instead of me working for it. Quite simply, that is my attitude towards everything. If I go into a situation believing it is bad, it will be. On the other hand, if I head into a situation believing I can come out a winner, I will win! That is why my definition of success is so important. You can be successful on any journey because you will learn something on every journey. You will gain a new skill for survival, you will meet new people, and you will always be further than you were when you started if you just stay in the race. This does not mean that you don't have to prepare for the journey in some way. It did not mean that I did not have to study or do my assignments. Instead, you do what is required with a positive attitude. You understand that the situation does not control you; you control the situation.

If you ask me, law school was not hard. It took a lot of discipline and studying. The worst time in law school was the week of final exams. But finals only came once every fifteen weeks. So, for the other 14 weeks you study and enjoy the debates! I had a great study partner named Leon. Leon and I were just alike! Our birthdays are one day apart. Our study habits clicked; so did our attitudes. We both just supported each other through each semester. We hung out together all the time. We took turns coaching each other in the race. Truth be told, Leon probably coached me more than I coached him. I did most of the typing of our outlines while he coached! We trained for the race together and always finished together. We graduated law school in the shortest time possible. We went year-round for two and half years.

In December of 1994, I marched across a stage for the third time in my pursuit of higher education. This time, I had completed my journey to justice. I was a lawyer. Well, almost. I still had to take and pass the Florida Bar Exam in February. Once again, I was joined by my family and friends to celebrate. A special person surprised me after turning my invitation down for my two previous graduations from high school and undergraduate; Mr. & Mrs. Miller were among the many well wishers in attendance! I was so glad to have her with me to celebrate the end of another race. And of course, the beginning of another race.

Leon and I had been faithful study partners for the two and a half years of law school. We planned our classes together as much as possible. It was no surprise that after graduation we started studying for the bar together. We graduated the first week in December. This left us eight weeks to study for the bar exam. Leon and I set up a serious schedule. In addition to taking the recommended Bar Review course, we were studying a minimum of eight hours a day the first four weeks. We had an outline of what we were going to study each day. The first few weeks were no different than our time spent studying for law school exams. We joked for a while, went home for breaks and came back to the library to hit the books again. The real test of both our friendship and future came three weeks before the bar exam.

The bar exam for Florida was going to be administered in Ft. Lauderdale, Florida. Leon and I decided that it would be smart for us to head south early. So, three weeks before the bar, we made the eight-hour drive to beautiful south Florida. We drove separate cars because each of us was staying in separate places in Miami. The schedule was set in stone: At nine in the morning be ready to be picked up. We took turns driving to a local university's library. We were staying about twenty minutes away from each other, so every other day it was my turn to go get Leon. On the opposite days, he would come to pick me up. We switched between St. Thomas University in Miami and Nova University in Ft. Lauderdale. (A change of scenery is always good when you are studying like a maniac.) Both campuses were beautiful. On most days, we preferred to study outside in the Florida sunshine. It seemed to suck out a little of the tension. Lunch and dinner were flexible. Neither of us had much money, so we usually hit a fast food restaurant. We would try to eat as healthy as a few dollars would allow. No mention of the law was allowed during lunch or dinner. That was a golden rule. On most days we would study until at least midnight. This routine was seven days a week for three weeks.

After the first week, I was feeling the pressure. We would review a subject in the morning, take a sample exam in the afternoon, review a subject in the evening, and take a sample exam that night. Our goal was to work up to eight hours of exam-taking by the week before the exam. The bar exam is two eight-hour days of testing in a huge civic center. The first day is the Florida portion of the bar exam. The second day is called the multi-state section. (This covers the national law.) There are four hours of testing in the morning beginning at eight AM. . You get one hour for lunch. At one PM, you head into the second four-hour segment of the exam. Needless to say, you must prepare for such a grueling schedule, not to mention making sure that you can keep two and a half years worth of material in your head from getting screwed up. A few weeks later, you take a four-hour exam on ethics. This was a race like no other I had entered.

My career depended on me being up to the challenge. The bar exam is only offered twice a year all across the country. Leon and I would try not to talk or think about the possibility of not passing, but it was on my mind. I started feeling the pressure of the fifteen-hour days. I started feeling the exhaustion of my body and my mind. My head would literally hurt from trying to stay focused. Tylenol became a part of my breakfast. By the second week, I could feel myself coming down with a cold. Leon admonished me, "V, you better not get sick now. We have got to keep studying. We can't take any days off!" I knew he was right. But my body and my mind were just tired. I had been in school for seven straight years. My mind wanted a break. My body was demanding a break. I knew I had to push myself to finish this race. However, finishing was not going to be enough this time. I had to pass the bar exam! I could not imagine putting all of this effort and energy into this exam to wind up not passing. I would die! Mrs. Miller was in my head telling me to find the strength within myself. It was hard.

One day during the morning study session, I was so tired I told Leon I had to take a nap. "V, you better stop playing around. Go get some coffee. Eat some sugar. But you are not going to sleep!" I snapped back, "You know I don't drink coffee, and I don't want sugar. I want to go to sleep!" The beautiful scenery was old now. The palm trees, sunshine, and nice breeze did nothing for my stress level. I put my head down on the table and fell asleep. I am not sure how long I slept, but when Leon woke me up

I knew it had not been long enough. I felt like crying! I could not keep this pace for another week and a half. How was I going to make it through the bar exam? Leon suggested we take a break to "walk it off." This was our signal to each other that we knew the other was stressed and needed an unofficial break to refocus.

I wanted to quit. I cannot describe what it feels like to want to quit, knowing you can't. My best shot at describing it is frustrating, physically sickening, and mentally numbing. My strength came from taking a practice exam and getting at least seventy percent right. That was my sign that maybe I would live through this nightmare! If I got less than seventy percent right, I would feel like screaming! I would be mad! I knew the material. I was dreaming about tort, constitutional, criminal, property, family and contract law! I could really care less about corporations and partnerships. I had no desire to practice corporate law. The hell with wills, trusts, and estate law! I started resenting the law. I had spent seven years in college; I had struggled all this time for what? To take a bar exam that would ultimately say whether I would be a "real lawyer?" This was bull! Don't even mention the $50,000 in student loans that would have to be repaid at some point. Sorry, tack on the $20,000 in interest and now we're up to $70,000 in debt before I ever get a job. The kicker is that getting a job depends on passing this stupid bar exam!

By the week before the exam I was drinking coffee everyday to stay awake. I was taking vitamin C like it was candy. A minimum of four Tylenol a day was standard. I could not sleep, despite the fact that my mind and body were exhausted. My mind would just race from one thing to the next: sample bar exam questions, where would I get a job, what if I failed, and what would everybody think? Three days before the bar exam, Leon and I took the two-day sample test. We acted like it was the real thing. At eight AM, we started the first half of the testing. No breaks until noon, except for a quick trip to the restroom. One hour for lunch. At one PM we started on the next four hours of questions. We broke for dinner at five PM. At six PM, we were grading the exam. Shortly thereafter, we would study the areas on which we had not gotten the minimum of seventy percent. There was no cut-off time because the bar was knocking at our door. We would stay at it until two or three in the morning.

The day before the exam, we met to go over the areas we knew had caused us problems. No practice exams, no fifteen-hour day. We took the first half of the day to just relax, which for me ended up being sleeping until time for us to meet. I had been staying with one of my sorority sisters during this time. However, the night before the exam I was to stay in a hotel by myself to make sure my mind was free from any outside influences. Leon and I decided the cut-off time that night would be ten PM. I drove to my hotel near the civic center, checked in, and took a shower. The last thing I did before I laid down was to call my pastor in Tallahassee. His wife was one of my sorority sisters. Both of them said a prayer with me on the phone. One of the things we asked for in the prayer was that my mind be put at ease. It worked because that night, I slept for the first time in weeks.

The front desk gave me a wake up call at 6:45 AM. I wanted to eat a good breakfast and to get to the civic center early. Leon called at seven. "V, you up?" "Yes", I said, "How about you? You ready?" "We will know in about an hour, won't we," he responded. We both just laughed, saying we would see each other at the center. I ate a good hot breakfast at the Denny's across the street from the hotel. I tried not to think about the exam. Instead, I read the newspaper. On the front page, I saw that one of my classmates at FSU Law School had been arrested for plotting to kill a professor. Well, that was unfortunate...but it sure gave everybody at the civic center something to talk about!

Leon and I were seated nowhere near each other in the huge hall. The test began with the administrator at the front of the hall explaining the rules. A few minutes later, we were asked to place two fingerprints on the exam. (Talk about security!) The big, red time clock started with four hours on it, then started counting down the first day of hell. I had done everything that had been recommended. I had plenty of pencils, a sharpener, cough drops and earplugs. I finished in about three and a half hours. I felt pretty good when Leon and I met for lunch. The golden rule was still in place...no talking about the exam on breaks. We ate at a nice restaurant on the water next to the civic center.

The afternoon session was not that bad either. I finished about thirty minutes early again. I was so glad I had made it through the first day. I refused to talk about the exam with anyone. Later that evening, Leon and I met for a review for the second day. Although I was tired, I felt good about my performance on the test that day. Leon and I met at the library after dinner around eight PM. We stayed until midnight. This was probably a mistake, because the next day I was really tired.

I got my wake up call from the front desk and from Leon again. I ate a decent breakfast with coffee, of course. Then, the same routine: the administrator giving her speech, the fingerprints on the exam, and the big, red digital clock at the front of the hall. I struggled through the morning session. I finished about twenty minutes early. That was still a good sign. I felt like I had done well, but I was worried about whether I could make it through the second half of the day. When Leon and I met for lunch break, my mind and my body would not cooperate. I went into the second part of the day tired, but trying to keep on track. I noticed I had to read some of the questions two or three times to comprehend. This was not a good sign. I finished the exam with only five minutes to spare. The pressure of the big, red numbers and then announcements every five minutes during the final fifteen minutes did not help.

You have to be a mathematician to figure out how the exam is graded, but they average the scores of the two days somehow. So, if you do better on one day than the other you can still pass. I left the bar exam praying that my first day and the morning of the second day would be enough to pass. I knew that I had not done my best in the afternoon session. I drove home that afternoon with tears swelling in my eyes. I did not want to take that exam ever again!

I received a job offer from the Orlando State Attorney's office when I got home. I had two weeks to pack up and move to Orlando. This pushed the exam results to the back of my mind. I started at the State Attorney's office on March 20th, 1995. The bar results don't come in the mail for at least two months. I was busy adjusting to a full time job, so when the envelope came in the mail I was somewhat surprised. Had time flown that fast? I was scared to see the results, so I waited until I got inside to open the envelope. I saw the scores. I had failed the multi-state by TWO points! There must be a mistake! My score on the Florida section should have been enough with this confusing averaging system to be a passing score. I looked over the numbers for at least fifteen minutes. Then I just started to cry. I was going to have to take this hellatious exam again!

I called Leon. He had passed. When I told him that I had failed by two points, he thought I was playing. When I started sobbing, he knew I was serious. For the first time since taking the exam, we discussed it. "V, how? You knew the material! You got eighty percent on the practice exams two days before!" All I could say was, "I know, I did know the material, but Leon, I was so tired the second day." Leon reassured me that it would be okay. He would call to check on me from time to time. He would give me the pep talks I was accustomed to. He would be my pit crew for this last lap around the track.

I say last because I was certified to practice law for one year after my graduation date. If I did not pass the bar exam in July, I would have to resign from the State Attorney's office. Talk about pressure! It was time for me to make a decision about the price I was willing to pay. I could take the entire exam over which the Florida Bar office suggested. Or, I could just take the multi-state portion over. Two days of hell verses one? Hard choice, right? The days were not the only consideration. It costs money each time you take the bar exam. I paid almost a thousand dollars to take the bar the first time. Now, I would have to pay a minimum of three hundred dollars just for the one day. The cost to retake the entire bar was close to five hundred dollars. I did not have this kind of money. I decided it was all or nothing. I had passed the Florida part of the bar. I would not take it again. One day of hell was better than two. I could do this! Well, if I found the money to register before the deadline, that is. My pit crew consisted of several friends. One of my best friends mailed me a check. It arrived just before the deadline to apply for the June bar exam. I said a prayer of thanks because I was at least entered in the final round.

My preparation for this final lap around the track was very different. I was working full-time. I had a full caseload. I did not have Leon with me to push me on the days I felt like stopping for a nap. But I had one powerful thing...my desire to win! Mrs. Miller was with me in spirit, telling me to discipline myself. I could hear her telling me, "You don't need a study partner. You have the potential, Veraunda. Apply yourself!" I developed a study schedule. I made an outline for what I could study each day. I went into my office an hour and a half early every morning. I would use that time to do practice questions. From seven to eleven at night, I would study. Two weeks before the exam, I took a leave from work. I spent eight hours a day at the public library or by the pool in my apartment complex. The office/clubhouse opened out to a beautiful covered patio. The rental agents kept an eye on me. They would offer words of support or encouragement every few hours.

If I wanted to go home and take a break, I would imagine Leon being there. A few stern words from Leon would put me back on track. He would call to check on me regularly. I would give him the status of my studying. The final week before the exam I only took sample tests. I simulated the testing environment...four hours in the morning, one hour for lunch, four hours in the afternoon. I would grade the exam after dinner. My rule was only two hours a night for reviewing my notes or covering material I had missed. I was doing well on the practice exams. My spirit was strong.

I took the day before the exam to relax. This time, the exam would be administered in Tampa, Florida. This is about an hour or so drive from Orlando. I drove over to Tampa after my mother stopped by to say a prayer with me. She gave me the money to pay for my hotel and gas. After a big hug, we both got in our cars. She was headed for work. I was headed for the starting line in Tampa. I was alone. I wished Leon was here with me. Well, he wasn't...so, I would have to make the best of it. I bought myself a lunch fit for a queen at a restaurant on the bay. After lunch, I treated myself to a matinee movie. By six PM, I was checking into the hotel. I watched television for a couple of hours, then placed a few phone calls. By nine PM, the lights were out.

The wake up call at 6:30 in the morning startled me. I had slept like a baby. No tossing and turning. No crazy dreams. I had rested peacefully. This was a good sign. Leon called to give me the final pep talk around 6:45 AM. I had a good breakfast, checked out of the hotel, then headed over to the convention center.

The set up was a bit different this time. All the people who were retaking the multi-state section of the bar were seated on the outer right hand side of the hall. I knew this because I heard several people around me talking about how many points they needed to pass this time. I turned around when I heard the guy behind me saying he had taken the multi-state twice before. This was his third time. My heart jumped! "How many points did you miss it by?", I asked. He told me the first time he missed it by two points, the second time by one. "You have got to be kidding me!", came out of my mouth before I knew it. I quickly apologized to him, because this was no time to be kidding about anything. The bar exam was more than a serious matter. But his statement had jolted me.

I had missed it by two points the first time. Maybe the advice from the bar to retake the entire exam was best. It was too late now. In ten minutes, the exam would start. The clock would start counting down the hours with big red numbers. I had paid the price to be here. I had studied. I knew the material. I was going to get my money's worth this time. I felt it! I just had one last piece of unfinished business to take care of. I turned to the guy behind me. "I am saying a prayer for you that this will be your last time around with the multi-state," I said with a smile. His response was simple, "I need it."

The preliminary instructions were given. The exam began with the big, red digital numbers 3:59 glaring at me from the front of the hall. To my surprise, I was calm and focused. I did not feel the anxiety like I had the first time. I took my time, read the questions, then bubbled in my choice. At 11:30 AM, I was walking out of the hall for the lunch break. I had finished thirty minutes early. This meant I was on track. I ate lunch on the bay again. By one PM I knew that I could win! My mind was so focused. My heart was peaceful. The questions seemed so familiar from the practice exams. Read, bubble, read, bubble. I did this for three and a half hours. At 4:30 PM, I was leaving the convention center, headed back to Orlando. I felt good walking out of the hall. I smiled to myself while thinking, "Girl, you jammed that exam!"

I got back to Orlando by six that evening. I called my pit crew to let them know I had completed the race. By the time I talked to Leon that night, I was convinced I had passed the exam. Two months passed. On September 19th, I received the letter. This time I did not wait until I was inside my house. I opened the envelope right there at the mailbox. It read:

"Congratulations! You have attained the passing grades on the Bar Examination and the Florida Board of Bar Examiners has recommended your admission to the Florida Bar. Your scaled scores on the July, 1995 General Bar Examination are set out below:

Part B Scaled Score   147.0

I had not just passed the bar exam…I had passed it by seventeen points! I was screaming and crying at the same time! I called the pit crew one last time. Leon's response was so typical of him. "V, I never doubted you would pass! Congratulations. Just remember me when you run for office." That was our little joke. Leon has always believed I am destined for some type of public office. I beg to differ. But then again…who knows what race will be next?

On September 25, 1995, Fifth District Court of Appeals Judge Emerson Thompson swore me in as a member of the Florida Bar. A few days later, I took the following oath in front of my family, friends, and co-workers, which by the way, included Leon.

I do solemnly swear:
I will support the Constitution of the United States and the
Constitution of the State of Florida;
I will maintain the respect due to courts of justice and
judicial officers;
I will not counsel or maintain any suit or proceeding which
shall appear to me to be unjust
Nor any defense except such as I believe to be honestly
debatable under the law of the land;
I will employ for the purpose of maintaining the causes
confided to me such means only as are consistent with truth
and honor,
And will never seek to mislead the judge or jury by any
artifice or false statement of fact or law;
I will maintain the confidence and preserve inviolate the
secrets of my clients;
And will accept no compensation in connection with their
business,
Except from them or with their knowledge and approval;
I will abstain from all offensive personality and advance no
fact prejudicial
to the honor or reputation of a party or witness,
unless required by the justice of the cause with which I am
charged;
I will never reject, from any consideration personal to
myself,

The cause of the defenseless or oppressed,
or delay anyone's cause for lucre or malice.
So help me God.

My journey to become a lawyer was complete. My journey to justice was just beginning, in reality. I would now be responsible for seeking justice on a daily basis. But that was a price I was more than willing to pay.

Apply the lesson in this chapter to your life:

Where is your journey headed?

_____

_____

_____

_____

Where are you on your journey?

_____

_____

_____

_____

Are you ready for the next phase of the journey?

_____

_____

_____

_____

Has your journey been worth it?

_____

_____

_____

_____

CHAPTER FIVE

How Much Can You
Bench Press

When I started law school, I also started working out on a regular basis. Florida State University had a beautiful student athletic center that had just been completed. The Robert E. Leach center was better than any Bally's I had seen. Glass windows stretched from the floor to the ceiling. There were three floors, all opening to the first floor. The building was spacious and airy. There were plenty of treadmills, step machines, bikes, weight training machines, an indoor track, an indoor pool, saunas, whirlpools, aerobic rooms, racquetball courts, and my favorite to watch…the free weight section. I liked to watch the men bench press! Why? Of course, the main reason was the physiques, but I also noticed they had a technique. I always smiled when I saw the process of bench pressing. It intrigued me that these men would attempt to lift such tremendous amounts of weight. I often thought they were crazy and wondered why they felt the need to lift so much, so many times.

If we are honest with ourselves, we are all bench-pressing something. The true question becomes why are we lifting it. The wisdom comes in knowing how much to lift and when to ask for help. The whole bench pressing technique is quite interesting. You take an amount of weight that you believe you can lift over your chest while lying flat on your back. Then you have spotters. These are the people who are usually friends working out with you. But on occasion, they are the coaches or trainers in the gym.

The spotters have several purposes. They serve as encouragers. I would hear the guys in the gym push the lifter with heartfelt words like, "You can do it. Come on. Push. One more time. No pain, no gain." The words seemed to have a powerful effect on the lifter. I would watch them moan and groan, but they would lift the heavy bar over and over at the coaching of the spotter. The spotter also serves to ensure that the weight does not become too heavy and injure the lifter. I would watch the spotters use their own strength in various degrees to help the lifter. I thought it was hilarious that a spotter would take a couple of fingers and act as if he or she was taking some of the weight off the lifter. I would think, "I know that little bit of help ain't doing a thing for the lifter." The times I believed the spotter was doing his job was when the bar was down to the lifter's chest and the spotter had to use all of his strength to put the weight back on its stand. Now that was impressive to me. The spotter was the hero! The spotter could lift as much as the lifter...that is strength. I thought the whole point of the exercise was to show off your strength. I was wrong!

One day, I decided I was going to try the bench press. I had been working out for a year or so, and I thought I needed to expand my workout routine. I chose to start when there were only a few people in the free weight section of the gym. I asked one of the staff members to spot me. I needed him to show me the correct method of bench pressing. The trainer started by explaining that you breath out as you are pushing up...the most strenuous part of the exercise, then inhale as you are bringing it down to your chest. Your hands had to be strategically placed on the bar. The weight had to be equal on both ends. But most importantly, the exercise should be done slowly to work the muscles to their full potential. It really did not look that complicated when I saw the guys bench pressing hundreds of pounds. I honestly thought it was going to be easy. I listened with a smirk on my face while the trainer tried to stress the importance of the lifting method and breathing. "This can't be that difficult," I thought.

When it came time to choose a weight, I did the natural thing...I asked the trainer, "What do you think I can lift? Where should I begin?" His answer surprised me because he said, "I don't know, it depends on your strength." What a dumb answer! I thought, "I don't know my strength, I have never done this before!" I verbalized my thoughts a bit more tactfully. "I have never done this before, so I don't know how much I can lift," I said. Again, his response shocked me. "The only way you will know is to pick a weight that seems manageable, then try to lift it." I was getting frustrated before I ever lifted a single thing! "Okay," I said, "Let's start with fifty pounds. I should be able to lift that without a problem." We put the weights on the end of the bar. I laid down on the bench. What a lesson I learned on the first push up.

Just getting the bar off the stand took strength! To bring the bar down to my chest without it hitting me took control and balance. However, to complete the exercise, you had to use the same strength, control and balance to get the stupid bar back on the stand. It really did not seem like the guys who were bench-pressing were going through all that I was just to lift the bar one time. But isn't that always the case? We always look at other people and say that we can do the same thing, or that it can't be that hard. Let me tell you, what you see is not always what it appears.

I am so tired of hearing people say that I am a strong woman! "But, Veraunda, that is a compliment." No, it is not because when people say that to me, I know they are not looking at how much I had to lift, or how many times I had to lift it. The guys who can bench-press hundreds of pounds started off with a lower weight and had to build their way up to several sets while increasing the weight week by week. If you stop for a period of time, you end up having to lower the weight and work your way back up. Strength in life is obtained the same way. Lifting crap over and over again. Taking more crap, lifting it, pressing yourself and having your spotters to encourage and push you when you just don't think you can lift anymore.

There are days when I don't want to be strong! There are days when I don't want to lift anything! There are days when I question what I am lifting and why! There are days when I just don't believe I have the strength that I need to lift the weight that has been put on my bar. What becomes interesting is when I allow others to put weight on my bar, and then I struggle to lift it while they watch and coach. I often wonder why they are coaching instead of spotting me. I want to yell, "Don't tell me I can do it…Help me do it!" If I am honest with myself, I allowed the weight to be put on my bar. I saw them coming up to me with the weight. In many cases, they asked me to take on the weight. The problem is, instead of saying, "No, I can barely lift what I have right now"; I try to show off my strength. By show off I don't mean parade around the gym saying, "Look at me and how much I can lift." On the contrary, it means being afraid to appear weak! I don't want to look like I can't do something. It is the same syndrome that I have mentioned on more than one occasion…I have something to prove…but to whom and for what?

When I looked at the guys in the gym bench-pressing, I thought it was amusing that they took on more than they could lift to impress the onlookers. I would smile while thinking, "Look at that show off. What is he going to prove? That he is stronger than he appears? What is the point of him lifting so much weight for others?" The real question became "Did the onlookers care one way or the other?" I answered the question for myself. Sure, I would be impressed for the moment, but I would move on to the next exercise quickly forgetting about the show off.

When I tried bench-pressing for myself, I discovered there were several stages. The more I lifted the weight, the harder it became. Let me explain. My theory on weight lifting was simple. The more I do, the easier it should get. Wrong answer! The first time I lifted the bar, I could do ten repetitions. (In gym language, this means do the same exercise ten times.) However, I could only do one set of ten. The next week, I did two sets of ten. It was not any easier to lift the weight; the secret was that I was building endurance and strength at the same time. Now, let me just take a minute to say that the physical pain was overcome by the excitement of being able to do more than I had the week before. I would wake up sore and aching after I increased the weight. But that was always a temporary feeling. It always went away within a few days. By the time soreness was going away, I was adding five or ten more pounds to the bar. After a few months, I was able to bench-press one hundred pounds. I felt like a champion weight lifter when I reached my goal of bench-pressing the big one hundred. During this time, I did not notice that the muscles in my arms and chest had transformed into cute little, tight muscles.

The whole bench-press process is a mental one. You make up your mind that you are going to try it. You realize it is not as easy as it appears. You have to make a decision about whether or not you will try it again. If you decide that you will continue, you must also set goals and decide what it is that you would like to accomplish through the lifting. The physical part of the lifting is the easy part, if you ask me. Once I had my mind made up that I was going to the gym, the rest was just a matter of lying on the bench and pushing the weight up and down. The problem came in when I did not feel like going to the gym. The days when I felt like I could not lift any weight are the days I really needed my spotters and coaches. There were days when the spotters would tell me how much I could lift. I would be tired or just plain unmotivated, but their words and their hand on the bar would help me get through the exercise. The spotters become real important in the mental process of bench-pressing.

Who are your spotters? Are they people that really want to see you develop strength and endurance? Or are they people who are jealous of your muscles? I have been blessed with dynamic spotters. My spotters vary in age, race, sex, and in their spotting methods. All are very effective and yet very different. There is no way I can have the same spotter every day that I am lifting. In life, you lift every day, whether you want to or not. Reliable spotters are a must for a successful work out. The spotter may depend on the weight that you are lifting. Are you lifting work, school, family, or friends? How many sets are you lifting at one time? Often, we are lifting several different weights at one time. Balancing the weights on both ends becomes crucial in bench-pressing. Where are your spotters in the balancing of the weight?

Mrs. Miller was one of my first real spotters from the outside world. Your family may or may not be able to spot you when you are lifting them as a weight. So, it is imperative that you have more than one spotter to help lift different weights. Mrs. Miller got me through the educational system with constant words of encouragement. There have been many other spotters during my journey that have a special place in my heart. These spotters were always an answer to a prayer for help when I could not bear the weight alone.

I can recall taking on the weight of the National Association of Advancement of Colored People (NAACP) Youth Council. When I started as the advisor for the council, it was twenty-five year old me, and seven kids. By the end of the first year, there were fifty kids. Within a few months of getting started, I was exhausted. The behind-the-scenes work of any type of community service is tremendous. My goal was to meet with the kids no less than twice a month. We met the first Saturday of the month in a formal setting. Parliamentary procedures were taught and used during the first hour, which was used for business. We would give updates on the previous month's activities, then move on to the upcoming activities. The last hour of the meeting was for educational enrichment, which included speakers, group exercises, or trips. There was at least one fun trip each month, which included activities like skating, horseback riding, bowling, dances, or movies. On average, we met three times a month. We were a busy group! I saw the Lord bless the youth council beyond my own belief in the three and a half years I was the advisor. But let me tell you, the weight was unbelievable during those years! I am a person who believes in conducting business in an organized and professional manner. At times, I believe that I add unnecessary weight to my life because I am a perfectionist.

A perfect example of how hectic the council could become is found in the work involved in a simple Saturday morning meeting. There was always an agenda. (Typed, of course.) There was a newsletter each month, complete with cute graphics and fancy fonts. There was a roll that had to be typed and updated after each meeting. (Attendance was the basis for rewards at the end of the year.) There was the collecting of funds for upcoming events. There was also the scheduling of the speaker or trip to follow the meeting, which always included several pieces of correspondence. Whew! I am tired just thinking of all the work that went into a productive meeting with the kids! But it was always worth the work.

At the end of the second month, I realized I needed help. There was no way that I could lift all of the weight by myself. I prayed, asking God to send me dedicated and committed help. My spotter arrived at the next meeting. Denise Jones had no idea what she was getting herself into when she decided to stay with her niece and nephew for their first meeting. But Mrs. Denise became one my best spotters with the council. At the end of the meeting, I approached her without knowing one thing about her and asked her if she would like to volunteer with the council. She agreed with no clue of how much she would be lifting. We became fast friends. I bet we talked on the phone three to four times a week coordinating, planning, confirming, and venting. Yes, venting!

The youth council was a part of the adult branch of the NAACP. However, the support of the president was non-existent. The executive board members would always have to vote prior to giving financial support or approval of our activities. Month after month, I would attend the meetings begging for support and help. I recall my first meeting, when an older gentleman told me that I was too young to lead the youth council. It is funny now, but at the time, I was offended. I set out to prove all of them wrong. I allowed them to put weight on me that I could not bear alone. Month after month, I argued and fought for new programs and funding. It quickly became frustrating. I dreaded going to the meetings. I left the meetings upset. Mrs. Denise and I decided that we would do it alone. We would lift the weight. We would endure. We got organized and boy, what a difference we were able to make!

A few months after we started, Valory Wheeler joined us as a volunteer. Her son, Marcus, was a member of the council. Once again, I had asked the Lord to send someone to help Mrs. Denise and me. I love how He answers prayers! Mrs. Denise and Mrs. Val were great spotters, although very different. Mrs. Denise was about my age, married with no children, soft spoken and, according to many people, looked like my sister. Mrs. Val, on the other hand, was close to forty, had a son, was single, and was great at whipping the kids into shape. My personality should be quite clear by now, but just in case, I was an outspoken, organized, married with no children advisor. The thing I admired most about Mrs. Denise and Mrs. Val, after three years of working with them, is that they always allowed me to be the leader. They did not always agree with me, but they always encouraged, supported, and respected me. That is the kind of spotting I needed in the council.

I am a strong willed and determined individual. But, I am not stupid. I know that I need spotters. I always tried to acknowledge their work in the youth council instead of taking credit for it myself. It was a team effort. You can't have spotters that you don't give credit to. Sure, you have a nice body or, in my case, a successful program, but what about all those days that your spotters lifted the weight for you? Hopefully, it is a two-way street. In the gym, I would see the same guys working out together. Each would take turns spotting the other. This makes perfect sense because they become stronger together. They may not be able to bench-press the same amount of weight, but they build endurance together.

There were several other advisors and parents that helped us lift the weight of the council. We all developed relationships based on our bench-pressing together. By the end of my three and half years, we were able to lift some amazing weight. I am most proud of the cultural diversity rally we were able to organize. It was a huge vision that came to me...find a big church and invite all races and denominations to have a great time celebrating our differences. The event cost over ten thousand dollars. We mailed over six thousand letters to sponsors and organizations. We did a massive publicity campaign to get the word out. I had never tackled anything like this before. But with the help of spotters, not only did the youth rally become a reality; it was a success.

Over one thousand people attended the rally. I was so overwhelmed by the completion of the project that my eyes filled with tears as I sat in the front row of the First Baptist Church in Orlando. I kept saying, "God, I can't believe that all these people are here. I can't believe that we got the T-shirts printed for the kids. I can't believe we have such a remarkable line-up of talent and speakers. I can't believe it!" Well, it was clear to me that the months and years of bench-pressing the youth council had paid off in a mighty way! We had added weight over years. Our goal became to expand and improve each year. That was no easy task, but we supported each other. We kept going back. We kept encouraging, we kept coaching, but most important, we kept lifting!

I have been active in many social organizations. I have been the leader as well as the follower. When I take on community service activities, I become over-committed at times. My inner voice will say, "Veraunda, you have more than enough on your plate. Don't do this to yourself." Then two or three people in the organization will tell me how bad the organization needs this or that or how this committee is really short. The next thing you know, I end up with more weight on the already stress-bent bar.

A perfect example is the year I took on the Paul C. Perkins Bar Association in addition to the NAACP Youth Council, a full-time job as a prosecutor, and teaching public speaking at a community college. The Paul C. Perkins Bar Association serves minority lawyers in the Central Florida area. I'll call it PCP for short. Several people had approached me about the position of president. I had said no each time, citing the youth council as a full-time job by itself. By the time nominations rolled around, I had been convinced by several people that they would spot me and that it would not be as much work as I thought. The good news is that I had a wonderful executive board that spotted me the entire year. The bad news is that I added more weight to my bar. There is no way to take on a new project, organization, or committee and not feel the weight.

Each month, I would meet with the executive board to determine the agenda. This was usually a lunch meeting downtown. I would get on my computer at home to draft the newsletter. Next would be copying the newsletter. Finally, I would take it to the secretary, Kimberly, so it could be mailed a week prior to the meeting. We rotated the meeting location each month. The vice-president, Jeff, was responsible for contacting local law firms to sponsor the monthly meetings and refreshments. The treasurer, Al, was responsible for making all the deposits and keeping accurate financial records. We worked well together. We were all young and excited about doing new things with the bar association. We wanted to take it to the next level.

We wanted to give something back to the community. So, we added more weight to the bar. Several of us had talked about giving a scholarship to an African-American law student, getting our constitution and by-laws recorded, while keeping all of the previous community service projects running. There were standard projects that PCP did each year: Thanksgiving donations to a local homeless shelter, Christmas toys for children at a homeless mission, a Las Vegas nite to benefit the United Negro College Fund, and a February Bar Luncheon speaker, followed by a reception for Black History month. These projects were not easy. You have to get the money. Someone has to coordinate the project. People have to volunteer to make the project come to life. Weight, weight, and more weight!

Time, in and of itself, is a weight. I found myself teaching two weeknights, running to meetings at least two other nights a week, and spending the majority of the weekend with the youth council. Somewhere in between, I found time to grade papers, create the newsletters, draft letters, and make phone calls confirming this program or that speaker. Thank God for the spotters! All of the projects were completed and successful...but it took the effort of numerous people. Sure, we received many compliments and praises about what a great year PCP had, but it cost all of us a price!

I spent very little time with my husband because of my involvement in community organizations. I was lifting so much outside of my home; I had no time left to lift my marriage or family relationships. I had no time to pursue or nurture meaningful friendships. So, many people commented on my leadership roles. "Oh, you are the president of PCP. Girl, you are really something! I don't know how you do it all: the youth council, the bar association, your job, teaching. You really have it together!" Truthfully, I have always been a good manager of time. But the reality check is that the positions and titles come with a high price...STRESS! I continuously worried about how this program would come together, if this event would be successful, or if the spotters would do their jobs to get me through this set.

I constantly felt like I had to be doing something every moment. I used my vacation time to attend conferences or conventions for one organization or the other. The lifting was all day, everyday. Bench-pressing can become overwhelming. I saw the muscles developing, I knew that my strength was increasing; yet I felt tired and weak. Strange? Not really. I knew that through serving others, I would reap great benefits. In fact, I <u>was</u> reaping great benefits. I was surrounded by sincere spotters who kept me grounded about who I was and why I was lifting so much. I really cared. I really believed I could make a difference. This may or may not be a good thing. I have strained muscles along the way. But as the trainer pointed out so eloquently, the only way to know how much I could bench-press was to put the weight on the bar, then try to lift it.

In our personal lives, most of us have people we call friends. Over the years, I have realized true friends are hard to find. When I worked out, I noticed a few guys would start out lifting weights together. However, by the end of the semester, the group would have lost one or two of the spotters. My guess is some of the spotters may have just come to the gym when they felt like it instead of when the friend needed them to come. Maybe the spotter just wanted to talk instead of really work out. There are many reasons that you must choose your spotters carefully. In a split second, the weight can become unbalanced or too heavy. If the spotter is not doing his job, you could wind up seriously injured. I have several friends that no matter what the weight, they will help me lift it. Of course, they each do their spotting in different ways.

Take Dashonya, for example. She is a beautiful, tall, thin, dark brown woman. She has a smile that just lights up your heart. I met Dashonya when I was a junior at FSU. We were both interested in becoming members of Delta Sigma Theta Sorority. I became friends with Dashonya about a year before we actually joined the sorority. I had no idea Dashonya would be such a strong spotter or a bench-presser. At first glance, she appears timid. Don't ever judge your spotters based on appearance!

Dashonya and I spent a lot of time together. We would shop, eat out, and just talk. We talked almost every day while we were in college. Dashonya became and remains one of my closest friends. I can tell her my inner most thoughts. I can cry with her just as quickly as I can laugh with her. A true spotter will always meet you at the gym when you need them. I was in the delivery room with Dashonya for the birth of her son, Jovan. It was one of the most special moments in my life. I have often thought about the strength it must take to birth a baby into this world. I held Dashonya's hand while she suffered through the contractions to bring Jovan into this world. I am not sure how much of a help I was to her during the physical pain, but I do know I was glad to be there with her while she was pushing. I was impressed by her strength.

Dashonya is not big on emotions. She is very composed and graceful. I, on the other hand, will cry in a heartbeat. The delivery of Jovan was typical Dashonya. I would have been screaming and crying. Not Dashonya. She just dealt with it. No complaining, no screaming, not a tear came out of her eyes. She just did it. I have wondered how she lifts all the weight she does. I have always admired her quiet strength. Sounds strange, doesn't it? Quiet strength?

Quiet strength means there is no complaining. No venting just to be saying something. No big show about how much you are lifting at the time. Dashonya and I have shared many things over the years. Sometimes, she shares after she has been through a tremendous amount of pain. I find myself wishing I could have been there for her as a spotter during the time she was lifting. But I realize I have learned a different bench-pressing technique from Dashonya. She has taught me that sometimes, just going ahead and lifting the weight without all the dreading; yelling, and screaming is just as effective. I love her for who she is. I love her for all the days she spotted me by quietly listening to cries of pain and hurt. But I also love her for all the victories she has shared with me. Each time I have reached a new level, Dashonya has been there. She was there for my wedding, for my graduation from law school, and for the Florida Bar drama. She continues to be here for me as my soror (my sorority sister), my friend, and my spotter.

I have to be honest. I will yell, cry, and whine through my bench-pressing. Does it help? I am not sure. Sometimes, it just feels better to get it out at the time…"This is so heavy, my muscles hurt so much, I know I am going to be sore tomorrow!" I have come to realize that being vocal helps me work through the weight. I think it through out loud. I want to make sure that my spotters agree with the technique. At times, I think I just need to hear the spotter's input to help me push the bar up one more time. There are not a lot of weights I have lifted alone. For that, I am thankful. But, I am learning about having that quiet spotter from within. I am learning to listen to my own inner voice when it says push, take a deep breath, or just rest for a minute.

Ruth Witherspoon, or Dean W, as I affectionately call her, reaffirmed the lesson of quiet strength that I started learning from Dashonya. I met Dean W when I applied to the Florida State University College of Law. She is the associate dean of Student Affairs at the law school. You talk about a bench-presser! This woman is incredible! I am not sure how many programs she oversees, but I can tell you her day to day load is tremendous. She is the director of the academic support program and the director of the pro bono (students must do so much legal community service for free). She oversees the following: all special testing, the peer advisor program, the tutorial program, minority law day, all scholarships, summer transition programs, first-year orientation, graduation ceremonies, and numerous other programs or projects. Add the weight of taking complaints from students, encouraging students, helping students find financial aid, and consoling fears about what happens after graduation, the bar examination, and job hunting. It is a bar full!

I will never forget the first time I met Dean W. One of my professors in the College of Communications recommended I go over and meet her prior to starting the Summer Law Program. I walked into her office without really knowing what I was going to talk about. When Dean W walked out of her office, I was a bit startled. She was a tall, beautiful black woman with gorgeous, thick, black hair. She was soft-spoken as she shook my hand and invited me into her office. I am not sure what I expected, but she sure was not it. I began the conversation with basic questions about law school. Dean W made me very uncomfortable during that first meeting. She had an eerie quietness about her. I found myself wondering what she was thinking. Why was she so quiet? Was it because I was talking too much? Was it because she didn't like me? Maybe she was just having a really bad day and I had caught her at a bad time. I did not know the answer. But one thing was for sure, I would not be hanging out in her office once I got to law school!

I have misjudged people on more than one occasion. My first impression of Ruth A. Witherspoon was way off! I left her office that day thinking, "She is too beautiful to be so mean." During my first year of law school, I discovered that Dean W was bench-pressing a tremendous load. The law school had about six hundred students, so it was fairly small. It was common to know almost everyone by name. I quickly realized Dean W was someone that almost everyone in the school needed in some way. Of course, I was one of those people!

Dean W is a great spotter for others despite having so much weight on her own bar. I guess you could say the majority of her day-to-day work is spotting students and faculty. Help lift this, help lift that, reassure this one, or encourage that one. All day long, students are in and out of her office with one crisis or another. I remember my first crisis in law school...fear! It does not take long for the fear of God to hit you in law school. Mine started almost immediately. I went to Dean W and it was at that moment that her quietness revealed its power. I was hysterical with tears and the whole works. But like Mrs. Miller before her, the quietness, the ability to just listen without emotions was soothing.

During the two and a half years I attended the Florida State University law school, Dean W spotted many times, in many ways. By my last year in law school, I was spotting her as her research assistant. I worked twenty hours a week in the Office of Student Affairs. I could not believe the amount of work the office generated. I was overwhelmed. Dean W was a strict and, very organized boss. By the time she asked me to come and work for her, I was very familiar with her quiet strength. Just her presence is powerful. I was afraid to take the position because I am so outgoing, jovial, and animated. In other words, the complete opposite of Dean W. I say this in a positive way because we really compliment each other. I worried about her thinking I was not serious about the position because of my jovial persona. I discussed this with her before I took the job. She shocked me once again when she responded by saying, "Veraunda, that is what I love about you!" In contrast, what I came to love about her was her quiet strength.

We are great friends now. It has been over seven and a half years since my first meeting with her. There is nothing I can not share with her. She has seen me at my worst and shared in my best. We spot each other well, in my opinion. I know there is nothing that she would not do for me. There is nothing I can say or do to make her love me any less. I cherish her because she continues to believe in my best, and encourages me to excel beyond my own dreams. There have been several times when she has said she admires me. I often ponder why. She has a great job, makes great money, has a beautiful home; if you ask me she has it all. But, as I now know, it all came to her through lots of quiet strength. I have learned so much from her about my bench-pressing technique. When she spots me, she exemplifies the type of bench-presser I want to become. I know she will meet me at the gym no matter what the hour of day or night.

I know that Dashonya and Dean W will lift that bar with me as many times as it takes to develop my muscles. They have met me at the gym late at night and early in the morning. I know they will always give generously of their quiet strength so I can look fit after a strenuous workout. I often wonder how I can repay them for the years of spotting they have done for me. I don't have the money, the house, or the position that Dean W has. I don't have much to physically give to Dashonya, either. But the one thing I do have to offer is my ability to spot them when they are bench-pressing. I will gladly meet them at the gym no matter what hour of the day or night. I will gladly encourage them to keep lifting and, when necessary, lift for them!

Over the years, I have had numerous spotters who have helped with various types or amounts of weights. All of those people have been instrumental in my developing the lifting technique and the muscle I have today. Some have pushed me in more aggressive ways. For example, I have one friend, who wishes to remain nameless, who has really helped me develop my character in the last few months. This spotter has said things to me in the most direct, yet supportive ways. They have been things I really would prefer not to hear about myself. Not because I think I am so great, but because they have forced me to really examine my techniques. Once you have been lifting for a long period of time and you are comfortable with your technique and weight, it is uncomfortable to try something new. Not to mention that your muscles begin to hurt all over again because they are getting stretched in a different way. This friend has said, "You may be uncomfortable for a while, but you need to reevaluate your lifting method". She flat out said, "The rewards will be tremendous if you are willing to readjust some of your lifting methods.

She has been stern with me and said, "Veraunda, you are controlling. You feel the need to be in control of the situation at all times." She is absolutely right. It is a coping mechanism many "strong" people use. We don't want to appear weak, so as long as we are controlling, or think we are controlling the weight we are lifting, we are fine. The minute the bar is off balance, or our spotters suggest something new, we try to get it right back under control.

As a result of this friend's comments, I have started to wonder why I feel the need to keep everything under control all the time. Several reasons came to mind in a short period of time. First, there have been times when I allowed a spotter to take control and they dropped the bar right on my chest. The pain was unbearable! I trusted them to lift the weight, or help me lift the weight. But because of their own weights, or in a moment of distraction, they left me in a position that not only damaged me physically, but mentally.

A prefect example is during some of my volunteer work. I have depended on someone to take care of a project, send a letter, or make a phone call. I believed in their word, trusted them to do their part and I was disappointed when they did not. My first thought was that if I had just done it myself, I would not have had to experience this let down. So, I choose to take on more weight because of a few bad spotters. Some of my experiences with spotters have caused me to question whether I should even continue to bench-press. At times, I have been afraid to go to the gym. I became afraid to pick up the bar for fear each spotter would disappoint me, let me down, or seriously injure me.

I am learning it is okay to trust spotters, but I need to choose them very carefully. Of course, I have my family as spotters. I also have spotters that are my colleagues, like Veronica and Helen. These are two of my lawyer friends who have spotted me in and out of the office. I have friends I have known for years like Patrice, Sandra, or Monica that have spotted me through school, relationships, or work dramas. I have my sorority sisters that will always support my efforts and lift me up in anyway they can. I am blessed! I have realized that there is no such thing as a perfect spotter. In fact, all spotters will have weaknesses. My challenge becomes to look for their strengths and call on them when I am lifting the weight I know they can handle. I have learned that spotters are all training, just like me. They are developing their own muscles. They are finding out how much they can bench-press, just like I am. I am learning to love each person for their strengths and not to focus on what they can not lift. We all develop muscles differently and at various times.

There is one other very important lesson I am learning...to know when to let go of the bar. My nameless friend has said to me a thousand times, "V, let it go. Don't pick it back up!" She continues by saying, "You lay it down, then you pick it back up." She was talking about a particular set of circumstances in my life at the time. But, I think the point fits perfectly with our daily bench-pressing. The circumstances I was facing were very difficult. I kept trying to lift the weight, knowing I could not. I tried everything I knew to make the situation better...talking crying, having fits, making threats, not talking, and pretending not to care. The truth of the matter was that I was trying to lift the bar with methods I knew would not work. I was desperate! I wanted the weight off my chest. The bar was just sitting on my chest. I could not breathe, I could not push, all I could do was just lie there, flat on my back, with this weight on my chest. I knew I could not lift the bar. I knew it was too heavy, but I wanted to be in control. The weight was not even mine to lift at times, yet I wanted to help out. I made matters worse. I strained muscles, cried doing it, and did not gain one ounce of muscle because I was lifting the wrong weight! Did I learn something from trying all of these different techniques? Yes! I learned when to let go of the bar! It has not been an easy lesson for me with my aggressive personality, but nevertheless, I am learning.

I am finally learning that even the best of athletes take time off to regroup. Professional athletes play for seasons, not all year long. They have set training periods to condition themselves for the season, and they have set off-seasons to rest and rejuvenate. There is no professional sport that lasts all year long. Hmmm…I wonder why? The answer is simple; the players would burn out or incur injuries. Everyone needs a break: the athletes, the trainers, and the fans. Bench-pressing is no different. There is a time to really push yourself and there is a time to take some time off from the gym. There were days when I would go to the gym to swim or ride a bike, instead of my normal routine. You must take time to rejuvenate. This does not mean you must stop bench-pressing. Instead, it means trying some different exercises, taking a day or so just to walk in the park or ride your bike on a trail. You don't always have to be in the gym lifting a bar to get a good work out.

I have learned over the years to be a bit more careful about increasing the weight too quickly. I have started evaluating the weight prior to lifting it. I have realized I don't have to lift everything everyone wants me to lift. I have learned the value of good, reliable spotters. I know it is all right to yell at the top of my lungs for help instead of letting the weight fall on my chest. I also know it is perfectly okay to take a day off from the bench-pressing to rest my muscles, to rejuvenate my spirit, and to allow my mind to relax. But, the key to successful bench-pressing is to continue to get to the gym, lie on your back, and lift the weight. Your commitment to bench-pressing will develop beautiful muscles, and a tremendous amount of strength will come in handy when you least expect it! You will be amazed at how much YOU CAN BENCH-PRESS...just keep lifting!

Apply the lesson in this chapter to your life:

How much weight are you lifting?

Who are your spotters?

Will your spotters meet you at the gym anytime of day or night?

Do you know when you are lifting too much?

Can you see the muscles developing from your bench-pressing?

Everything Has A Price

CHAPTER SIX

RESPECT IS EARNED,
POWER IS PERCEIVED!

After about eight months in a felony trial division, I met my match. He was a Fifth District Court of Appeals judge filling in for a trial judge in Orlando. This had to be a life lesson in the making because I was normally assigned to one judge. However, there were four prosecutors assigned to each judge. It was not uncommon to be farmed out to a judge who had finished his/her docket and was willing to help with a trial from another division. Since I am still a prosecutor, I will not name any judges. I will refer to this judge as the Appeals Judge.

I will never forget my first day in front of the Appeals Judge. I had on a nice suit, complimented with sling-back heels. I was ready to go to trial. The case was a fairly simple one, in my opinion. The defendant had been accused of armed trafficking in cocaine. The police had pictures of the crack cocaine, nicely packaged in over sixty little clear baggies. We had the gun in evidence along with the cocaine and baggies. I had the crime analyst from the Florida Department of Law Enforcement with her chemistry background to testify that the substance in the baggies was cocaine. What else did I need? This defendant was facing a minimum of three years in prison just because of the firearm. I was prepared to send him!

I had done my homework. I knew the facts of the

case. I knew the officers and the chemist. I was ready; at least I thought I was ready. I am a cheerful person by nature. Anyone who knows me will tell you that I love to smile. This day was no different for me. I walked into the courtroom pulling my briefcase on what we affectionately call our flight attendant carts. I said hello to the court deputies. I said a bright good morning to the trial clerk. The court personnel are your best friends in this business. They can make your life easy, if you let them. Most of them have worked in the courthouse for years. They know the ropes. If you listen to them, you can learn something. I should have listened this time because they were trying to prepare me for a day from hell. One court deputy was an older lady. I called her Mrs. Mary. She took good care of me when I practiced in her courtroom. On this day, she told me that I was going to be in for a treat...the judge did not like long jury selections. She warned that he would just interrupt in mid-sentence. The judge, according to the trial clerk, Kim, was a harsh one; a real barker. The other court deputy agreed with her while telling me that I would be fine. I was always prepared. I shouldn't have much to worry about. In reality, I should have been worried the minute that the judge took the bench.

The judge came in, sat on the bench, and leaned over with his glasses on his nose. "Is the State ready to proceed?" he asked in this deep, authoritative voice. "Good morning, your honor. I am Veraunda Hubbard on behalf of the State...." Before I could finish, the judge gave me his first bark. "The question was not who you are counsel...the question was, 'is the State ready to proceed.'" I am sure that my face had a weird look on it. I know the clerk and the court reporter were looking at me to see how I would respond. I know this because I was staring at them in disbelief. I was also looking at them to gather my thoughts without making it obvious that this judge had rattled me. I responded with a simple, "Yes, your honor, we are." The judge declared, "Fine. Madame Clerk, if you would call for the jury."

The court deputies went over to the jury room to escort the members of the potential jury back to the courtroom. This took about five minutes. During this time the lawyers would normally discuss some preliminary matters with the judge and look over the jury questionnaires. The questionnaires give you basic background information on each potential juror. Employment, age, sex, marital status, prior convictions or lawsuits, was all standard information on the form. By the time the jurors arrived, I was ready to go. At least, I thought I was ready to go. When the judge acknowledged my opportunity to speak to the jurors, I stood up, walked over to the podium confidently, and introduced myself.

I started as I always did. "Good morning, ladies and gentlemen. My name is Veraunda Hubbard and I represent the people of the State of Florida. It is really important that each of you answer out loud so that the court reporter can type your responses. He can not record head shakes, nods, uh uh's or ah hah's." The court reporter looked over at me with an appreciative smile. I continued, "I am going to ask some questions that may be personal. If at any time you feel uncomfortable answering them in the open, just let me know. We can approach the bench with the court reporter to discuss the answer."

I continued, "Let me just start by asking general group questions. How many of you here have ever been stopped for a traffic infraction? Will you raise your hands for me, please?" I was the first to raise my hand, as I have been stopped three or four times. The jury was smiling and chuckling amongst themselves. All but one person raised his hand with me. That is when the judge cut in. "Mrs. Hubbard, I will not allow that question!" I was not sure why he would not allow the question. It was a valid question that is used by many lawyers to inquire about the feelings of the jurors toward police officers. It is not uncommon for someone to have a bad experience with a member of law enforcement that may cause him or her to dislike law enforcement officers.

The point of jury selection, believe it or not, is to find fair and impartial people who can listen to the testimony and make a decision at the close of the trial. I gathered my thoughts and moved on without missing a beat. I asked the next question. "Does anyone here know anyone in law enforcement: a relative, perhaps a neighbor or friend?" Several members of the panel raised their hands. The judge clipped in again. "Mrs. Hubbard, I will not allow that question." A few more questions; different issues with the same response. Okay, now I was getting the point. This judge was not going to let me ask much of anything. I tried to get as much information as I could, with the judge barking at almost every question. Within ten minutes, I was taking my red trial notebook back to my table saying, "No further questions, your honor." I was rattled and flustered.

Most judges give lawyers leeway in jury selection. Not this one. I was going to have to pick my jury from the questionnaires, which are not all-inclusive and surely do not tell you about individual biases that may prevent a juror from being impartial. The defense lawyer's fate was the same as mine. I think he asked, or should I say tried to ask, three questions before he gave up and sat back down next to his client. The defense lawyer had been practicing over fifteen years compared to my two and a half years. I looked over at him. He was just as flustered as I was. To be honest, I think the jury was, too. We had done jury selection in less than fifteen minutes. This was probably a world record.

The witnesses were told they had forty-five minutes to get to the courthouse. This meant that when the judge asked me to call my first witness, I had a problem! "Your honor, jury selection went quicker than I had anticipated. My first witness should be on his way, but I gave him forty-five minutes to get here," I informed the court. The judge barked back, "Mrs. Hubbard, I asked you at 8:45 this morning if you were ready for trial. You responded in the affirmative. Now, at 9:15, you are telling me you are not ready for trial?" How do you respond to that question when your assigned judge gives you about forty-five minutes to get your witnesses to court from the time the case is called?

Here I was in front of a substitute judge who obviously had a different policy, yet I had no way of knowing it. I was told at 8:30 that morning that I would be in front of this judge, with no time to find out his policy on calling witnesses. I could only respond by saying, "Your honor, the witnesses are on their way." By this time, I was really flustered, but I was trying not to show it. My voice was shaky. My eyes were watering, but not because I was hurt or embarrassed. The water in my eyes was because I was mad! I was mad that this judge was trying to make me look like I did not know what I was doing. I was mad that he was doing this in front of other people. Finally, I was mad because there was nothing I could do about it!

Mrs. Mary, the court deputy, was sitting behind me. She gave me a warm smile as if to say, "Don't let him get the best of you." The judge knew he had me and he played on it. "I want to see counsel in my chambers immediately!" The judge exited through his private door into his chambers. The court personnel gave me a look that said, "Ooooh, you are in trouble!" The defense lawyer asked me what we had done. Of course, I had no clue. The defense lawyer and I entered the chambers not knowing what to expect.

"Have a seat counsel," the judge said in a totally different, human kind of voice. "Mrs. Hubbard, you are upset with me." I responded through watery eyes, "No, your honor, I'm fine." I was lying and he knew it! He then said that he knew his reputation preceded him. That reputation was one of harshness, he went on to explain. By this time, I was blowing my nose on tissue from the judge's private restroom. The judge went on to tell me that the courtroom is a stage and the judge and the lawyers are the actors. This was after he barked at me for the entire jury selection process. "Mrs. Hubbard, I was acting. You are also an actor, as is the defense attorney. It is our job to make sure we give a great performance. The courtroom is a stage, Mrs. Hubbard." The man who was talking now was not the man that was on the bench barking at me. He seemed like a grandfather talking to his grandchildren about the theater. I was at odds with this statement because, as a prosecutor, my job is to seek justice, not put on a show. However, I knew he was telling the truth to a certain extent.

The presentation is just as important as the information. Before our little chamber conference was over, he apologized to me for upsetting me. (I still insisted that I was not upset.) The trial started as soon as my officer got there, about fifteen minutes later. Things went fairly well after our little chat in the chambers. The judge, or shall I say actor, gave the lawyers only fifteen minutes for lunch. I decided to stay in the courtroom and work on my closing argument. I had finished with all of my witnesses. After lunch, the defense lawyer chose to proceed with his side of the story.

No more barking from the bench occurred after the conference in chambers. I thought I had done a good job, especially considering how the morning started. During the fifteen-minute lunch that the court deputies and court personnel shared with me, I was teased. The trial clerk, Kim, acted as if she were crying...a more dramatic replay of the morning, in my opinion. The court deputies joined in with laughter. The court reporter, a sharply dressed black man by the name of Bobby, smiled his million dollar smile and said, "Mrs. Hubbard, don't you worry about a thing. Girl, you handled your business!" All the court personnel then agreed that I was probably going to get a conviction. They were right.

The trial went so well that the defendant pled just after lunch instead of facing a conviction at the hands of the jury. The judge sentenced the defendant to the maximum sentence, just as I requested. The kicker to this whole thing was when the judge came back in the courtroom after our fifteen-minute recess. He saw that I had not eaten. "Mrs. Hubbard, I have half of my sandwich in my office. Would you like it?" I wanted to ask him if he were out of his mind. But instead, I smiled and said, "No, thank you, your honor. You might try to poison me." The courtroom personnel burst out in laughter. To my surprise, so did the judge. I love my job!

My official title is Assistant State Attorney for the Ninth Judicial Circuit of Florida. Whew! That is a mouthful. I am currently assigned to the sex crimes and child abuse unit in my office. Most of my cases involve children who have been abused by adults who are family members, neighbors, or friends. I serve at the pleasure of Lawson Lamar, the State Attorney for the Ninth Judicial Circuit of Florida. Mr. Lamar is an elected official. My boss has been in a military intelligence unit, a prosecutor, the Sheriff of Orange County, and now he is the keeper of justice for Orange and Osceola counties. I can truly say it has been my pleasure to serve as a prosecutor, or as we are called up north, district attorney.

As a prosecutor, I have tried over a hundred cases. Each case is unique. There is nothing like putting on a suit with some heels, add a scarf for effect, and letting the show begin. There is a thrill in being a trial lawyer that I love. Your heart beats, and your mind is scrambling, trying to think of what the defense lawyer will argue BEFORE he argues it. Of course, no one knows what a jury will do until they come back with the verdict. So, when I go into a courtroom, I want to impress while representing the State of Florida as if I were Lawson Lamar himself.

As a communications major, I look at each trial as a public speaking engagement that has a lot riding on my ability to persuade a jury. That is why my background is so important. I paid the price during a long educational journey. Today, that education is paying off. I have a great job, I feel good about what I do, and I have enough money to pay my student loans back each month.

The cost of being a prosecutor varies. I don't make as much money as I could if I were working in private practice. I am a prosecutor twenty-four hours a day, seven days a week. That includes in the grocery store, the mall, the movies, or a restaurant. I run into jurors, defendants, parents of defendants, victims, witnesses, co-workers, and my students on a weekly basis out in public. We have court deputies in each courtroom, complete with firearms. My office has investigators that also are armed. But when I leave the security of the courthouse complex, I am just like any other citizen. So, how I treat people becomes essential to how they will treat me outside the courtroom. It is my hope that each day I am earning respect.

Earning respect is a simple concept. This is my personal definition of respect: Strive to be professional, human, and fair. Please notice that perfection is not mentioned in my definition. Instead, it is replaced by the word 'human', which means we will all err on many occasions in our lifetime. I often joke about this in my classes with speech students or law enforcement recruits. I tell them in the beginning, "I am not perfect. Don't be surprised if I mess up. In fact, expect it. Then when I do, you are not disappointed." I say this with a smile because so many people put public servants on pedestals.

The public, our friends, and our families make us

out to be super people. Take it from me, it is hard to live up to other people's unrealistic expectations on a daily basis. The titles that come with our positions seem to imply that we are successful just because we work at a certain place. Just the fact that I am a lawyer seems to both impress and intimidate people. Then, when they find out that I am a prosecutor, it really puts me in a different category. I understand that I am blessed with a very serious job. However, I am a human who can only do her best on a daily basis. The title does not keep me from feeling the range of emotions that come with winning or losing. The title does not wipe away a victim's pain or give them the courage to testify. The title does not scare away bad guys or keep them from committing crimes. The title is just that...a title! A title to which other people give too much value or power.

In my speech class, I teach the concept of power. Perceived power is how others perceive you or your position, then determine how much power they will give you. This is where we come back to the word respect. In most cases, if people respect your position, power will follow automatically. Let me share another courtroom experience to make my point.

At one point in my career as a prosecutor, I was assigned to a felony division with a very difficult judge. This was a male judge with a very bad temperament. He made my life hell for the year that I was in his division. When I started in the division, I was warned by co-workers, defense attorneys, and court personnel that he and I would clash. I had not had any problems with judges in the three years prior to this assignment, so I could not imagine my fate. I respected judges. I followed courtroom protocol. You know, stand when a judge enters the courtroom, stand when speaking to a judge, etc. I always addressed the judge as 'the Court' or 'Your Honor'. Sure, there were times when in the heat of battle I would argue my position aggressively.   However, I had never intentionally disrespected a judge.

The morning started at 8:30 with basic docket calls. In English, this means the clerk would start calling the cases as they appeared on the judge's daily calendar. I had a sentencing scheduled on a case that had pled earlier in the month. My victim wanted to be present to make a victim impact statement. In the state of Florida, a victim has the right to be present at all proceedings and has the right to make a statement to the judge prior to sentencing. Somehow, this case was set on the docket for 8:30 and 1:30 on the same day. I had called my victim asking her which time would be best for her. She responded that the 1:30 time would be more suitable to her work schedule because she could take her lunch hour to attend the sentencing. "No problem," I told her, closing the conversation with the directions to the courthouse.

What I thought was a simple docket error that would work for the benefit of my victim became a huge problem. When the judge called the case at 8:30, I gave a brief explanation of the history of the case, then informed the judge that the docket also had the case listed at 1:30. I explained my victim's situation and that opened the door for the following exchange of words:

The Court: "Mrs. Hubbard, did it occur to you that you should have called my judicial assistant to inquire about the two times listed?"

Me: "No, Judge it did not. I was under the assumption that since the case was on the docket twice and either time would be appropriate for the sentencing."

The Court: "Well, I am calling the case now for the sentencing."
Me: "My victim works downtown and can be here within

fifteen to twenty minutes, if the Court wants to proceed this morning. I just need a moment to call her."

The Court: "The victim should have been notified to be here at 8:30."

Me: "I spoke with the victim yesterday, and as previously stated, I asked her which time would be most convenient for her. The 1:30 time worked best for her."

The Court: "Mrs. Hubbard, I did not ask you what was convenient for the victim..."

By now I am losing my patience. I really do not see what the big deal is. However, the judge continues to go round and round with me for a few more sentences. I shift into a 'keep your mouth shut' mode, because if you allow this man to upset you, you will be the one getting in trouble. So, I start looking in the file as if it is the most interesting file I have ever seen. I let the judge continue on his little spat. I refuse to comment when he asks me questions. I am smart enough to know that no matter what response I give, he will not be satisfied. So, I just ignore him. Why did I do that? Let's pick up the dialogue here:

The Court: "Mrs. Hubbard, do you hear me talking to you?"

Me: "Yes, Judge, I do, but I have answered all of your questions. I told you that I could have the victim here within twenty minutes. No matter what I say, it is not going to be good enough, so I am just listening to you."

I immediately go back to looking at the file as if it is a best selling novel.

The Court: "Mrs. Hubbard! I am sick and tired of your attitude. I am tired of you rolling your eyes and ignoring me! I AM DEMANDING RESPECT!"

This was it! My supervisor tried to keep me from responding, but I had taken his position and abuse of power for the last time. I stood up, put my hand on my hip, looked him dead in the eye, and said the following:

Me: "You don't demand respect! YOU EARN IT!"

The Court *(who is now standing up while pointing across the courtroom at me)*: "Young lady, you are this close *(using his thumb and forefinger to show me how close I was)* to being held in contempt of court!"

Me *(with both hands on my hips now!)*: "You do what you have to do, but as I said, respect is EARNED!

The courtroom was silent. The court deputies, Ed, Jamie, and Danielle, were staring at me as if to say, "If the judge says cuff you, we will have to do it...but we really don't want to." The judge was steaming. So was I. I stared at him with a look that said, "I am not afraid of you, so do what you have to do." His face had turned red. He threw a couple of files on the bench, then called for a ten- minute recess while storming out of the courtroom.

As soon as the judge left, the twenty or so people in the courtroom started clamoring amongst themselves, probably in disbelief. A couple of lawyers came over, giving me high-fives while stating, "You go, girl!" I might be going in ten minutes...to jail for contempt of court. But, I was willing to pay the price for my words. I had said them with everything in me. I meant them with every breath in me. The court deputies came over and started joking with me about how they were going to cuff me, then put me in the holding cell. This was no laughing matter to me. Yet, to those who had witnessed my stellar performance, it was hilarious. My supervisor was present for the whole episode. She was telling me in her sweet, calming voice that before the judge could hold me in contempt, he would have to hold a hearing.

The ten minutes seemed to last an hour. I feared that during the recess the judge was stewing over what to do with me. Finally, the judge took the bench with a silent, but anxious, courtroom watching. We were all waiting for the verdict: Was Veraunda going to be held in contempt of court? If so, what would the penalty be? The judge had a few choices. The judge could fine me. (Not like I had the money to pay it!) Or he could hold me in a jail cell. From my point of view, jail was much worse than any fine. But, I was willing to pay the price for my heartfelt words. My mind was racing through the possible sentences when I heard the judge tell the clerk to call the next case. What? Call the next case? Much to my surprise, not to mention relief, he did nothing! Absolutely nothing! Well, except to order me to have my victim there at 1:30 PM.

Despite my anxiety in this situation, nothing happened. Correction: almost nothing. I had earned respect by standing up for myself. Several of the people in the courtroom that day secretly gave me high-fives, or supported my willingness to say, "Enough is enough." The people who were supporting me were glad that I had the courage to stand up to the judge. Standing up to the judge was a risk. However, by this time, I understood he had only so much power over me. He could only have as much power as I LET him have over me. I had GIVEN him much more power over me during the previous months.

I did not realize this until my trial partner, John, brought it to my attention one day. John and I were perfect trial partners. Opposites do attract. John is a handsome,

FBI-looking white guy, who has the most level temperament of anyone I know. I can count on two fingers the number of times I have seen him upset...not mad, just upset. It was not uncommon for me to consult him for advice when I was on the border of wanting to choke the judge or anyone else for that matter. John always had a way of bringing me back down to earth. He was good at refocusing my attention back on reality. On this particular day, I was whining to John about how sick and tired I was of the judge talking to me this way, or treating me that way. Without looking up from his desk, John plainly said, "Veraunda, why do you let him get to you?" Good question. No answer was needed.

I allowed the judge to upset me. I gave him the power to rattle me. I allowed him to edge me into battles that I did not need to fight. I allowed him to be the topic of my conversations day in and day out. The popular phrase that knowledge is power is an understatement. Knowledge can change your life! Once I *knew* that I was giving the judge too much power in my life, I stopped it. I realized what the problem was. It wasn't him. It was me! Imagine that! I *could not* change the judge. I *could not* make the judge do anything. But, I *could* change how I responded to him. I *could* stop talking about how sick and tired I was of his treatment. I *could* ignore his smart remarks. I *could* accept him for who he was. I *could* acknowledge that he had a very limited role in the massive world of my life. I *could* focus on his positive attributes like his efficiency in running a courtroom, his superior knowledge of the law and, most importantly, we almost never had court on Fridays. Believe it or not, I *could* earn his respect.

I was transferred out of his division a year later as a part of a normal office rotation. (My office tries to rotate attorneys so that we have the opportunity to work in various areas, which helps prevent burn out.) I was extremely glad to be going to a non-trial division called intake. In intake, there are several attorneys who review the cases as they come in our office to determine which charges should be filed. The intake attorneys do not go to court on a regular basis; it is more or less an office job. Despite the change in my attitude toward the judge, intake was a welcome change for me. I saw the judge about a month after I was transferred. I was walking down the street at lunchtime when he approached me, asking how my new assignment was going. I told him that I really liked working in intake because it was a nice break from having court everyday. His response was a total surprise, yet the ultimate compliment. "But, Veraunda, you belong in the courtroom. With your talent, any law firm in town would hire you." I was speechless...which does not happen much. I had earned his respect. Truth be told, he had earned mine as well!

You can earn respect based on many character traits: honesty, courage, diligence, or hard work. I have tried to exemplify all of those traits. I try to keep a positive, cheerful attitude in a stressful and a difficult profession. At any given time, most Assistant State Attorneys are processing over one hundred cases in different stages. Often our witnesses are not cooperative; sometimes this includes our law enforcement officers. We are working with secretaries who are over-worked, under-paid, and under-appreciated. We work long hours during the week, come into the office on weekends...I even have the computer accessible from my home. It is hard to keep the big picture in focus on some days. "There is more to life than work."

I often wonder where to draw the line. I have had some really big cases in my career as a prosecutor. I would toss and turn the night before. My mind would run through the case over and over flushing out all the possibilities. My stomach would be so nervous that I could not eat breakfast or lunch. But at the end of the trial, when the jury delivers the verdict, my one hope is always that I earned their respect, regardless of the verdict. I have no real power when it comes to their verdict. They are six citizens with different backgrounds, different beliefs, and different values. I have less than an hour to question a panel of up to sixty people about these backgrounds, beliefs and values. The defense and I have to come up with six people that we both agree on. Now, the defense is hoping that the jurors will rule in their favor. On the other hand, I am hoping they will deliver a verdict in my favor.

My title as an Assistant State Attorney means that I have the burden of proof. I have to prove beyond a reasonable doubt that the crime happened. The defense, on the other hand, does not have to prove one thing. So, where is my power? I have to use my mouth as a tool of persuasion. I don't choose my victims or my witnesses. Unlike on television, it is unrehearsed and un-staged. No big surprise confession from the audience has ever occurred during one of my trials. I present the evidence to the jury, then wait for their verdict. I have to accept and respect their verdict even if I don't agree with it. I can not change the jury's decision. I have no way to guarantee that they will interpret the evidence as I would like for them to. However, I can prepare my case, I can speak to the witnesses, and finally, I can present the case in a competent manner. Outside of that, I have no power over the outcome.

It is always amazing that after I finish my closing argument I feel a sense of satisfaction. Strange word to use, huh? Well, I use the word satisfied because I know that I have done my best, I have worked hard, prepared diligently, and done all that was within my power to see that justice was served. I realize that the jury will have to use their power to determine guilt or innocence. Once I have done the closing argument, I can't do anymore. My power ends at that moment. The case is out of my hands. I don't torture myself with what I could have done differently or that I should have said this instead or that. It is a complete waste of time to second-guess myself at that point. I have no power to change what has been done.

I'll be honest. When the jury comes back with the verdict, my heart beats fast hoping for a guilty verdict. But, I also know that they have made a decision. I have to respect that decision. I respect the fact that they are doing their civic duty. I respect the fact that they listened during the trial. But most importantly, I respect that we, as humans, don't and won't always see things the same.

One of the most difficult cases that I ever tried involved an eight-year-old boy who was sexually molested by his seventeen-year-old neighbor. The facts were fairly simple, in my opinion. In order to protect their true identity, I will call the eight-year-old, Billy and the seventeen year old, John. John was like a big brother to Billy. He played with Billy, was trusted by Billy's mother, and friends with Billy's brothers. He violated that trust by sexually molesting Billy on several occasions. John threatened Billy, so he never told. We found out about the abuse by a twelve-year-old neighbor who saw John touch Billy inappropriately while riding bikes. We'll call him Tommy. Tommy told his dad. That is where the journey to justice began.

I met with Billy for an initial interview. He was the cutest little boy. He was very mannerly, answering my questions with 'yes ma'am' or 'no ma'am'. He was embarrassed that he was talking to a woman about what another boy had done to him sexually. I tried to reassure him that everything would be all right without promising him that John would be sent to prison for the rest of his life. I don't make promises in my job. I have no power over the other people involved in the court system, so I can't promise what they will do. I do have power over what I tell my victims or their parents. I do have power to keep them grounded in reality, which is often not what they want to hear. I also have the power to be ethical in my position as a prosecutor. So, I tell the truth (which is supposed to be the cornerstone of justice) in hopes that no matter what the outcome of the case, I would have earned the respect of the victims, the court personnel, and the jurors.

Billy's mother was very cooperative with me. (Believe it or not, many parents of victims are not.) She was always pleasant, yet concerned. I would have been, too. This case involved her next-door neighbor. It involved a child that she had considered one of her own; a child that she trusted with her most precious gift...her youngest child, Billy. To top off all of the emotional trauma, the media had picked up the case. There were stories in the newspapers and on television. Of course, the community was torn. My advice to her was simple: "Focus on your son, he needs us to remain grounded during this process. We have no power over what people will say, but we do have power over how we react to it."

It took almost a year for the case to go to trial. I charged John as an adult with three counts of sexual battery on a child less than twelve years of age. In Florida, John was facing up to life in prison. After conferencing with Billy and his parents, we made a plea offer of fifteen years in prison followed by 15 years of sex offender probation. John rejected the offer. It was Billy's word against his; he was willing to take the risk. I was ready to go to trial.

I had gone over this case with a fine-tooth comb. I had every statement highlighted and tabbed. I wore my red suit with a nice scarf...this is my power color. Red? Yes, red! It is bold, yet confident. It signifies that I am ready for blood in the battle! It means, "Look at me; pay attention, I have something to say. You have no choice but to listen!" It says I am confident, creative, but most importantly, I am competent! I was ready for the challenge. Seeking justice is a battle that is won or lost in the mind of the soldier. My mind was made up...this was going to be the performance of a lifetime. I had tried other high publicity cases, but Billy had touched my heart in a way that only an eight-year-old could. I could not sleep the night before the trial. I really believed that John would seriously hurt Billy if he were released. I had to do everything within my power to protect Billy.

The cameras were rolling, the tape players recording, the reporters were writing, while Billy told the jurors how John had violated his trust, had threatened to hurt him if he told, and had done unspeakable things to him sexually. Everyone, including myself, listened with undivided attention. It was different hearing it from Billy on the stand. John was sitting at the table with his lawyer. Billy was talking about the seventeen-year-old boy sitting right there! John was close to six feet tall. He had the build of a football player. I looked at Billy who was small, skinny, and scared. I could see John on top of Billy. I prayed that the jury could, too.

Tommy took the stand next. His testimony was chilling. One day, he was riding his bike with Billy. John walked up to the two boys, then grabbed Billy's bike by the seat. Tommy was shocked when he saw John put his hand inside of Billy's shorts. Tommy was twelve. Tommy testified that he did not know what to do. Eventually, he gathered enough courage to tell his father. His father testified that he had never seen his son so traumatized as the night he came in the bedroom to speak with him. I saw the trauma as Tommy relived the events on the witness stand. I prayed that the jury did too.

Billy's mother testified near the end of my case. She had not been allowed to sit in the courtroom with her son. There is a rule of evidence that says if you are a witness in the case; you cannot be present while other witnesses are testifying. (This is to prevent witnesses from just repeating what someone else said or changing their story to be consistent with other witnesses.) Billy's father had never been told the details of the abuse. I feared that if he sat in the courtroom, Billy might freeze. I suggested Billy pick family members that he felt comfortable with to sit in the courtroom. He picked his older brother and his aunt. No one is allowed to discuss the testimony of the witnesses other than the lawyers until the trial is over. This means I could only tell Billy's mother that he had done fine when she asked about his testimony. This woman was just trying to hold it together by the time she took the stand. She testified on the third day of the trial. She had been sitting outside in the "Halls of Justice" for three days. She was ready for this journey to justice to be over. The exhaustion was on her face. John's betrayal of her trust was evident in her choice of words.

She struggled to hold back tears as she described Billy hollering for her from the bathroom on one occasion. She remembered with painful guilt that there was blood in Billy's stool. Having three boys, she thought nothing of it at the time, and dismissed it as constipation or a short-lived virus. When she found out the dates of the abuse, one was around the time that she had seen the blood. She was devastated. As she testified, I could see she just wanted to turn back the hands of time and take Billy to the doctor. Then, perhaps we would have had medical evidence of the abuse. I could feel the love she had for Billy. I could sense the feeling that she had let him down by not doing something when he reached out to her for help. I prayed the jury could feel it too.

When the mother was about to step off the stand, the judge made a mistake. This was his first day as a Felony Circuit Judge. He was very nice, but unfortunately, this was his first sexual battery case. He instructed the mother to wait a minute. He told the jurors that she was a very important witness, then asked them to take a moment to think about whether they had any questions for her. The jurors started talking amongst themselves. Before you know it, the defense asked for mistrial! Oh, my God! How was I going to explain this to Billy and his family? The judge did something that caused the jurors to discuss the case prior to going back for deliberations. This is forbidden by the rules. UHHHHHHHHHH! I had lost three days of sleep and had barely eaten. Now, I had to tell Billy we were going to have to start all over again!

I went out in the hall. I know my face showed every emotion that I was feeling: disappointment, frustration, and exhaustion. I tried to choose my words carefully. *"Guys, I need you to trust me. Can you do that?"* Billy came over and held my hand. His smile faded quickly when he saw my face. My tone said it all. Billy's mom asked me what happened. I had to tell Billy, Tommy, and their parents and family members that we were going to have start over. Billy's mom burst out with a rage that I had never seen before. It scared me. Foul words could not express her anger. I understood. But, now was not the time to lose it. Billy was squeezing my hand as the situation erupted. Billy's dad was stating that he would take care of this situation. He did not need the court system...to hell with it! I had to act fast. Billy did not need to see this!

I quickly told Billy's brother to take him outside. He did as I instructed without questions. I took Billy's mother by her shoulders, squared them to me, then firmly stated:

"You can't do this! We have to be strong for Billy. If he sees you like this, he is not going to testify again. He is going to think HE did something wrong or caused this situation. In reality, Billy never told because he was scared. If I don't know anything else, I know that children react to their parents' emotions. We, as adults, must make it okay for Billy and Tommy. We are going to hug them

129

and tell them that they did a great job; that we are proud of them; that they are brave little boys and we need them to come back one more time to make sure that John never does this to any other little boy again. Mom, Dad, this is a journey...we take it one step at a time, but we do it together, knowing that justice demands that we trust her!"

The tears in the eyes of Billy's mom made it clear she had gotten the message. The rest of the family also got the point. WE MUST FINISH THIS JOURNEY TO JUSTICE. The family had only one question..."Can we have a different judge?" Normally, the answer would be no. However, the judge in this case felt so bad that he asked a more experienced judge to hear the case for the second trial. The media ran the story headline: MISTRIAL!!!!!! I had only one comment, "The family and I have agreed to finish this journey to justice."

The case was reset for trial two months later. I found out I was being promoted. This meant I would be relocated to another office. (We have three separate offices throughout the circuit.) My heart sank as I picked up the phone to call Billy. I explained that a new prosecutor would be assigned to this division. I wanted to help in any way that I could. I suggested a meeting between me, the new prosecutor, and Billy to make the transition. I gave the family the opportunity to discuss the matter. When Billy's mother called me back the next day, the conversation was heartbreaking. "Veraunda, Billy said he will not talk to anyone but you." I sat silent...tears in my eyes.

I didn't know what to say. I was being promoted; this office was thirty minutes from my new assignment. The trial was at least a four-day trial. What would my new judge say about me coming back to try a case during the first week of my trial period with him? I would have to talk to my supervisors. This was the first time a transfer had ever held such a dilemma for me. In the seconds that all this ran through my mind, Billy asked his mother if he could talk to me. God, why does he want to talk to me right now? Maybe in five minutes I will be able to hear his little voice without wanting to melt inside. Before I knew it, she had handed the phone to Billy. "Mrs. Veraunda?" I mustered up the voice to say, "Yes?" He continued, "You told me we were going to do this together, now you are leaving me. I can't talk to anyone but you." I made a promise before I could stop myself. "Billy, I am not going to leave you, I promise! I will come back as long as you promise me that you will tell what happened one more time." I heard the relief in his voice as he said, "I will! I promise!" My heart was overwhelmed.

It was clear to me that I had not only earned Billy's respect, but I had earned his trust. He had brought me a flower everyday of the first trial. He had given me a hug every morning. He believed in me. He did not understand that the real power belonged to the jurors. As I started the second trial, I had a theme: "Journey to Justice." It was a reminder to me that everything had a price! Trying this case twice was very difficult. I was willing to pay with everything I had for Billy to see justice.

Before the trial started, he gave me a little bracelet with two hearts that he won at the fair. He told me that he had spent his whole allowance trying to win it. As I prepared for work the first day of the trial, I put on that bracelet while saying a prayer. "Lord, You have got to let justice be done in this case. This journey has to be finished for Billy. Please give me the strength, wisdom and words to demand justice." My prayer was simple because I understood I had no power.

The four days passed by quickly. All the witnesses had been through this before. The cameras rolled, the tapes recorded, the reporters wrote. One by one, over three days, each witness told his story again for the new jury. I had my closing argument prepared. The judge ended court for the evening. Closings would be given first thing in the morning. I could not sleep! I got up at one AM. I paged my detective, who worked on the case. He was still up, putting down some tile in his house. I asked him if he could listen to my argument. He said sure. By the time I was finished, he had reassured me, it was a winner. I hoped so. This was my last chance to make a difference in this case. My words had to be powerful!

As an instructor of public speaking, I tell my students that you have to do four things as a speaker:

1. Your audience has to want to listen to you.

2. If you get them to listen, then you want to make them think.

3. If you get them to think, you want to make them feel what you are talking about.

4. If you get them to feel, you can get them to act.

Well, this closing argument had to have all four elements. It was a nasty subject with a high cost for everyone involved. John was looking at up to life in prison. Billy was looking at the end to a long nightmare of abuse. Tommy needed to be rewarded for doing the right thing in a difficult situation. For the jurors, it was a question of society. John, Billy and Tommy all depended on them to do the right thing in a difficult situation.

There was no medical evidence presented. The doctor who performed the exam explained that because the abuse was not reported immediately, the physical trauma would have healed prior to his examination. My words had to cover every argument that the defense would throw at the jury. I had one premise. If the jurors would just travel with me and Billy down the Highway to Justice, when we reached the end of the journey, the price they had to pay would be clear. They would have to find John guilty. The power was in their hands. The choice was theirs.

Would they be willing to pay the price for justice?

I prayed one last time, then said these words: (This is an abbreviated version of my final argument.)

Ladies and Gentleman of the Jury, when I first introduced myself to you, I told you that I represent the PEOPLE of the state of Florida. Today, the PEOPLE are seeking justice! The PEOPLE are seeking justice for Billy and for Tommy! We have been on a long, hard, traumatic journey. Today, this journey can end with justice. This journey can bring peace to two little boys. This journey can reward Tommy for doing the right thing in a difficult situation. This journey can confirm for Billy that good does prevail over evil! I invite you to go back with me, go back with Billy, and go back with Tommy to the beginning of this journey.

As with any journey, we must first outline or map out our trip. We need to identify our destination. We will start with the logical place...the beginning. We will travel toward justice. As with any trip, we will see signs that confuse us. We will see side roads or alternative paths that we can take. Perhaps these alternatives appear to be short cuts that will save us time, or perhaps these short cuts appeal to us because there is less traffic on these roads. But as we travel, we discover that these paths have led us nowhere! In fact, they have wasted our time. They have all been dead ends. At some point, we are forced to return to the main highway...which brings us to our destination of justice. This is where we can finally rest. This is where we can get a feeling of satisfaction and a sense of accomplishment because WE made it! Despite the delays, the stormy weather, or the feelings of not being able to continue at times. Won't you come with me as we go back to try to make this journey to justice together?

Our first stop on this journey is the facts. The facts are simple and have remained constant during this trial.

On one occasion, John lured Billy over to his house to play video games. After they played the games, John pulled Billy's pants down, then sucked his penis in the living room. John threatened Billy, stating that if he told, he would beat him up.

A few months later, John invited Billy over again, this time for a surprise. John told Billy the surprise was in his bedroom. When Billy entered the bedroom, he was thrown on the bed, then John sodomized him. Once again, Billy was threatened. John told him if he told, he would hurt him.

John had his last strike at the end of that same month. While Billy and Tommy were riding bikes, John grabbed the seat of Billy's bike. He then put his hands in Billy's pants while Tommy was watching. Tommy was so disturbed by what he saw that he told his father, which led to the involvement of the judicial system.

We have encountered several side streets on this journey. The defense took us down "Only Kids Street." This is an interesting street because here we are asked to discredit the testimony of Billy and Tommy because "they are only kids." The law requires that you weigh everyone's testimony the same, unless you are given a reason to do differently. The evidence in this case supports the "kids."

Billy told his mother about the blood in his stool. Billy's mother noticed a change in his behavior, but could not explain why, despite trying to identify what caused this change. Billy did "kid's stuff" on the stand, which directs us to his credibility. He yawned quite a few times, he slid down in the chair while I was speaking to the judge at the bench, and he appeared tired at times. He stretched while being spoken to. The really important question is, "Where did Billy, who is just a "kid", and Tommy, who is just a "kid", get these facts?"

How would an eight-year-old "kid" know about white stuff coming from a male's penis if he had never seen it before? This same "kid", when asked what it was, said it was like pee but sticky. I asked him if pee ever came out like that. He said no. I asked Billy if he had ever seen his brother's or father's pee look like that. He said no. This "kid" still does not know what that "stuff" was.

How would an eight-year-old "kid" know about sucking other boys' penises or being penetrated in the rectum? How would he be able to associate pain with being sodomized if he had not felt it? Why would a twelve-year-old kid make up a story of seeing John put his hands in Billy's pants? There is no evidence of independent knowledge on the part of either boy to support that these children would have any reason to know about any of this stuff.

Why would the "kids" make this stuff up? So they could come to court to tell a room with over thirty strangers, including media cameras and reporters, about being sexually abused? Or perhaps it would be to put their family through a very traumatic experience...no, wait! It would have to be so that Billy could take a medical exam where your knees are up to your chest, with the doctor probing your rectum.

To insure that "Only Kids Street" has the full ride...even if Billy made this up, why didn't HE ever tell if he wanted attention? HMMMMMMM? Billy never told. It was Tommy that broke the golden rule in the house of not waking his father up to tell what he saw John do. Ladies and gentleman, this is not good attention. It is bad attention.

All of the adults describe the boys as being visibly upset and embarrassed when they talked about what happened in this case. Billy shook when he told his mother. Billy has never told his dad all the details of the abuse. If Billy really wanted attention, or to get John, he could have told his brothers and had John beat up. Billy is a "kid" who has been traumatized by the actions and threats of

John. Billy has done what we would expect a "kid" to do...he was scared silent!

The next side road we encounter is "Doctor's exam neither proves or disproves" Road. Here we meet up with the head of the Child Protection Team. He tells us that he has examined over 3,000 children for sexual abuse. He also told us that it is extraordinarily rare to find any evidence of oral union with a penis. The doctor told us that it is very seldom that you find physical evidence of penal/rectal penetration. He said that even within a two-day time frame, physical evidence would be slim. Why? Because the rectum is a forgiving organ. It is elastic in nature; it stretches to a large size. He gave an example of the bowel movement of children being larger than an erect, adult male penis. Yet, it returns to the original size within a short period of time. We recall the testimony that there have been cases where the doctor has seen photographs of a penis in the rectum. He performs a physical exam with no physical findings.

This is where we run into snow on our journey! We talked about circumstantial evidence in jury selection. If it looks like snow, feels like snow, and the surrounding circumstances have convinced you that it's snow, then it's snow! Here we did see the snow. Tommy saw the snow when he witnessed John putting his hands in Billy's pants. Billy's mother saw signs of the snow when she observed blood in Billy's stool during this time period. Billy felt snow when he felt pain from John putting his penis in his rectum.

As we get back on "Journey to Justice" Highway, we realize that getting off the path is easy to do, but it is even harder to continue the journey when you are tired, frustrated, and traumatized! At times, we start to wonder whether we should have even taken this journey to begin with. I imagine that this is what Tommy felt while struggling with whether to tell. I imagine that this is what

*Billy felt not being able to tell. I imagine this is what Billy's mom must have felt realizing that her son would be subject to interviews with several strangers and a trial that might possibly be the most difficult thing she would put her son through in his lifetime. I imagine that when the media showed up they all felt like quitting, giving up this journey, asking themselves why should I keep going? Their strength, their hope, their faith, came from one word...**Justice!** Justice will be their peace. Justice will end their journey. Billy made an interesting comment to the detective. He said, "I don't want to get John in trouble, I just want him to leave me alone." Billy is seeking peace today! He is seeking an end to a horrible nightmare. Tommy is seeking peace and closure today! He needs to know that he did the right thing by telling the truth! He needs to know that as citizens, we have an obligation to speak out against wrongs and to fight for those who can't defend themselves. The most important message that you as jurors have the power to send today, is that when kids do the right thing they are not going to be let down or called liars, just because they are "kids!"*

Billy was on the stand for two hours without a break. He answered questions. He stayed on the path to justice, despite the fact that he was restless. He was being asked the same questions over and over. He was unsure of certain big words. He asked for questions to be repeated a couple of times. He pushed forward to justice. Now, Billy is depending on you as a jury of his peers to help him finish this journey to justice. He is depending on you to do the right thing in a difficult situation, just like Tommy did. Billy is depending on you, just like the PEOPLE of the state of Florida are, to end this horrible nightmare and to finish this journey with Justice! Justice has been delayed;, please do not allow it to be denied! As a representative of the PEOPLE of the state of Florida, which includes Billy and Tommy, WE are confident that you will return the only

JUST verdict...GUILTY of three counts of sexual battery on a child less than twelve years of age. Thank you.

As I walked to my seat, I looked at Billy. His head rested on his mother's shoulder. With her arm wrapped around him, he was safe. He was also asleep. The last four days had taken their toll. He couldn't sit through an hour or so of closing arguments. I understood. Billy's mom gave me a thumbs-up to signal that she thought I had represented her family well. I took one look over at the jurors; several were wiping their eyes. GOD! I know they listened to me. I know they are thinking. I also know that several of them are feeling. All I need for justice is for them to ACT! A few of the jurors looked back at me. Their eyes seemed filled with exhaustion, yet I saw a look of hope. I can't explain in words what happens when you give that closing argument. But it is an emotional plea. They felt it. So did I. I had made it clear. The power was in their hands. I sat down. I realized that I had been shaking and tears had swelled in my eyes.

The jury went out on that Friday afternoon about three PM. They had not reached a verdict by six PM. The judge decided we would resume deliberations on Monday at 8:30 AM. The waiting is the hardest part. Parents and victims ask for your opinion. "What is taking so long?" or, "What does it mean if the jury takes a long time?" The answer for me is always, "I don't know." That is the truth. I have no clue what is going on back there in that small room. I always bring some work to keep myself occupied. Time is valuable in this business. No need to waste it on guessing or second-guessing myself.

Monday morning at about 8:15 AM, I saw one of the male jurors walk in with a dozen Dunkin' Donuts. I wanted to know what that meant. Did he think it was going to be a long morning, or was it just a kind gesture on his part? On this morning, Billy and his family looked rested. The weekend offered a much-needed break for all of us. Billy gave me his ceremonial hug. He told me that he had missed me over the weekend. His mom said that he was so glad to get outside to play with his friends, for a change. She, on the other hand, was glad for some peace and quiet in the house. I had gone to Disney World on Saturday, to relax. I wanted to forget about this trial for a few hours. Sunday, I slept the majority of the day. A four-day trial will drain everything out of you.

Billy and I started talking about his weekend. He told me he had something special for me. I smiled because everything he had given me was special. He had done a wonderful job. He had treated me like I was a queen. I watched as Billy started digging in his pocket. He pulled out a little silver key. It was about the size of a quarter. It was a fancy key. The kind that opened little fancy jewelry boxes. I gave Billy a big hug while saying thank you for the beautiful key. He surprised me because he asked me if I knew what the key belonged to. I had no idea. I tried guessing. Maybe his car? There was a big laugh from Billy. "Mrs. Veraunda, you know I can't drive! No, it is the key to my heart! " I was melting fast. He had touched my heart with that statement. I fought back tears while giving him another big hug. That jury better not let him down, was all I could say!

Two hours later, the court deputy came out into the hall to announce that the jury had reached a verdict. It was about time! Billy ran to me and grabbed my hand. His mother stood right next to him. The rest of his family, which included Tommy, crowded into the courtroom. John also had family present. The courtroom was tense. The media sat in the back of the courtroom, cameras rolling, tapes recording, pens ready to write. The judge announced that the jury had reached a verdict. I had given my usual instructions to the family: "No matter what happens, please try not to scream or yell. The court deputies will remove you from the courtroom if there is any kind of disruption. If you feel like emotions are going to overtake you, please hurry outside of the courtroom to release them. When you are composed, you may come back in." (If this jury did not come back with a guilty, I might need to leave the courtroom!) I hate this part!

Judge: *All rise for the jury. (Jury enters)*

Judge: *You may be seated. Ladies and gentlemen of the jury, have you reached a verdict?*

Foreperson of the Jury: *Yes, your honor, we have.*

Judge: *Would you hand the verdict form to the court deputy, please?*
(Foreperson hands over the envelope which contains the verdict form to the deputy. Judge looks at the form to make sure it is filled out correctly, then hands the form to the clerk.)

Judge: *Madame Clerk, would you publish the verdict.*
(My heart is pounding; I look directly at the jurors. I will face them with the confidence that I did a good job. I have left justice in their hands...now, I will find out what they did with it.)

Madame Clerk: *We the jury, find the defendant as to count 1:* ***GUILTY*** *of attempted sexual battery on a child less than twelve years of age.*
(My heart feels relief...but my mind is questioning why the jury came back with a lesser included offense. I am also questioning what this means as far as a sentence is concerned. How much time will John get now with the lesser charge?)
Madame Clerk: *We the jury, find the defendant as to count*

*2: **GUILTY** of attempted sexual battery on a child less than twelve years of age. We the jury, find the Defendant as to count 3: **GUILTY** of battery.*

What? I did not understand this verdict...so, the jury believed that John only attempted to sodomize Billy? Were they saying that John only attempted to suck Billy's penis? Finally, the battery means that they found no sexual touching during the bike incident...just that John touched Billy against his will. I had to get a grip fast. The most important thing was that John had been found GUILTY on each count. I looked back at Billy, he was hugging his mother who was crying. I also looked at John who just hung his head low. His parents were also crying. The reporters were writing with a fury.

The judge then proceeded to ask each juror if this was his or her verdict. Each said it was. The judge thanked the jurors for their service, gave them some closing words, then excused them from the courtroom. I went back to hug the family after the jury exited the room. I would explain the verdict when we were done. (At least I would try.) John ended up with only nine years in prison. The judge followed the prison sentence with twenty years of sex offender probation.

Was justice served? I thought so. More importantly, Billy thought justice was served. I am not sure he understood the entire process. But, he understood the word guilty. He understood that John was going to prison for what he did to him. He understood that nine years was a long time. He understood that in nine years he would be seventeen. Tommy also understood. His courage had paid off! All the reasoning of the jurors did not matter to these boys. John was going to be punished for doing a really bad thing to Billy. Justice had been served!

The press swarmed around the parents. (Kids cannot be taped without their parent's consent.) The parents denied interviews to protect their identity. The families asked me to make a comment for them. It was simple; "Justice has been served." I walked with the family to the parking lot. Billy's mom sung praises on my behalf to my supervisor, who had come over for the verdict. Instead of listening to her comments about me, I was saying goodbye to Billy and Tommy.

Billy finally broke my heart. "Mrs. Veraunda, am I ever going to see you again?" I couldn't fight the tears this time. I was devastated. I was speechless! I mustered enough strength to say, "Billy, I don't know if you will ever see me again. But I want you to remember how proud I am of you. I want you to know that I will always have the key to your heart with me wherever I go." Billy gave me a really hard hug. "Mrs. Veraunda, I love you! You kept John from hurting me again." All I could say was, "Billy, John is going away to prison for a long time and it's because you had the courage to tell those jurors what happened to you. You helped me keep John from hurting you. I could not do it without you, sweetie."

I saw Billy's mother out of the corner of my eye. She was watching us. She walked over to me, gave me a huge hug and a warm smile. "Mrs. Veraunda, we just could not have made it through this without you! I know Billy couldn't! I really trusted you. When Billy said he wouldn't speak to anyone other than you, I knew we were going to be okay. I knew he trusted you. Thank you for coming back to do this case." My supervisor was still standing there. I looked over at him as if to say, "Help! This is just too emotional for me!" He just gave me a warm smile that reassured me that it was okay.

I asked Billy's mom to keep me posted on his progress. I warned her that counseling was important in the healing process. It was my attempt to change the subject while preparing for the final goodbye. One last hug from the boys, a thank you again from the family, and Billy was gone. I have never seen him again. I have thought of him often because I keep the little silver key in my wallet as a reminder of how important my job is. The key is a constant reminder that I have the power to make a difference in the lives of others.

How are you using your power? Many people just waste it. They waste their power on situations that they can't change. They waste their power on people that they can't change. The real power is in how YOU cope with these situations and people. Are you abusing the power you have by trying to control others? Are you abusing your power by talking to people in inappropriate ways? Yes, how you interact with others is a form of power. A simple smile from you is such a powerful tool. Through that smile, you have the power to make someone's day.

Power is perceived. How do you perceive yourself? What do you perceive your power to be? How do other people perceive you? Are you giving YOUR power away to people who should not have it? Are you using your power to control your mind, your reactions and your attitudes? People can perceive your passion for truth and your desire to do the right thing. People can perceive your quest for personal growth. People can perceive your motivation to help others. People are willing to give you respect when they perceive you are using your power in a positive manner.

When I finally started realizing that the only person that I have the power to change is ME, life started becoming easier. This is a daily lesson. I can't give what I don't have. If I don't have the power to control myself, how can I share any power with others? I can share my struggles now, because I recognize that they made me stronger. The struggles with myself are the most important ones I can fight. I have the power to win those battles. I have the power to control myself. People can and will respect a hard worker. People can and will respect someone who is willing to pay the price. I am constantly amazed by a simple premise. First, you must be passionate about working on yourself. Then, you must be passionate about using your power to help others. As a result, people will perceive your power and YOU WILL EARN THIER RESPECT!

Apply the lesson in this chapter to your life:

Where is your power?

_____

_____

_____

What are you doing with your power?

_____

_____

_____

Who are you giving your power to?

_____

_____

_____

Are you earning respect or demanding it?

_____

_____

_____

EVERYTHING HAS A PRICE

CHAPTER SEVEN

MOMENTS IN LOVE

I have a strong suspicion...
that much that passes for constant love
is a golded-up moment walking in its sleep.
— *Zora Neale Hurston*

May 23, 1992, was one of the happiest days of my life. I had everything I could dream of, or should I say, everything I could afford. I started out the morning with a friend cooking a wonderful pancake breakfast. I left home around ten in the morning to finalize the decorations.

The event of my life was taking place with the backdrop of nature hosted on a ten-acre estate. A man-made pond sat picture-perfect in the middle of the land. On one side of the pond was an island with a bridge connecting it to the land. A gazebo had been built on the peninsula overlooking the water, making it the perfect centerpiece of a ceremony. A bridge that Derek had labored on for hours straddled the middle of the lake, right next to the gazebo. A family of wild migrating ducks completed the scenery. I had dreamed about this moment since I was a little girl...my wedding day.

I had met a man that I was willing to spend the rest of my life with. This man took my heart to new levels of love and trust. His name was Derek. We met in the oddest place. One night, as I pulled my bus into the parking lot of Taltran, there was a new face and body directing me to my spot. He was a nice dark brown. The lines in his stomach were a sign that he worked out. But his arms...mmm! His arms and legs had muscles! He was at least six feet tall. He had soft brown eyes. His face was stern. He was indeed a handsome man.

I had thought of everything. I knew from my childhood days in the park, that I would have an outdoor wedding. Nothing compares to the beautiful sun, the greenery of the trees, the reflection created by the water, or the sounds of birds chirping without a care. Nature reflects how awesome our creator is. The ten-acre estate of a relative was perfect, not to mention inexpensive.

To fulfil the dream, I needed a horse-drawn carriage, a long white gown, a pretty crown for a headpiece, a beautiful cake, and an audience of almost two hundred guests. I shopped for over a year to ensure that everything was picture perfect. I planned the entire wedding myself for over a year and a half. Every detail was logged in a wedding notebook.

I had rehearsed the day in my mind over a hundred times. I even had a theme picked out years before I knew I was going to get married. The theme was "Moments in Love." "Moments in Love" is a beautiful instrumental song performed by the musical group Art of Noise. The first time I heard it, I knew it would be my wedding song. The blend of the instruments, the beat of the music, and the pattern of the melody make you feel in love...at least for the moment.

After a few months of seeing him at work, Derek surprised me with his romantic side. On our first date, we drove out to the National Forest. It was beautiful. The edge of the forest sits on the Gulf of Mexico. The St. Mark's Lighthouse was the first one I had ever seen. The waves crashed up on the rocks as Derek and I had our first picnic. We listened to the sounds of the turbulent sea. We watched birds make their nest in a nearby tree. There was a peace that only nature can provide. The evening sun crossed the sky. Hours had passed. Derek took my hand in his. His soft eyes seemed to search my soul. His smile warmed my heart. At that moment, I knew I was falling in love. Derek must have felt it, too, because he started to speak after what seemed like an eternity of just looking at me.

The moment was perfect! His lips were moving; I could hear the words very clearly, "I love you." I felt my heart rate increasing fast. My mind said that this was an out-of-body experience. I heard my voice saying, "I love you, too." I felt his strong arms around me. I felt his lips meet mine. This was our first "Moment in Love." The date was January 16, 1989. I had just turned nineteen.

The guests started arriving an hour before the ceremony. I was tucked away in a two-story hotel suite. I took a long bath. I put on Beautiful by Estee Lauder. It was one of my favorite perfumes. I carefully put on my pantyhose with little wedding bells on the ankles. I wrapped my housecoat around me while my hairdresser started styling my hair. The suite was somewhat quiet. A few sentences here or there to break the silence would cause nervous laughter among the occupants, who all understood that a wedding day is sacred.

I let my mind wander back over the past two years with Derek. A smile crossed my face as I remembered the second time we went to St. Mark's Lighthouse. It was a cold, crisp morning. I had awakened to a teddy bear holding a big read heart waiting for me. The bear had a little card attached. It read, very simply, "Will you marry me?" Derek's eyes danced with excitement as he told me to get dressed before I answered. We had somewhere to go first. I got dressed quickly. We started driving out of town. I knew where we were going. I looked over at Derek. He was special. When we arrived at the entrance of the forest, memories of our first date scrolled through my mind. We parked near the lighthouse.

It was freezing. The water crashed against the rocks and the wind from the sea beat my face. Derek took my hand in his, then knelt on one knee. He pulled the heart that the bear had been holding from his leather jacket. The heart opened and inside sat a little gray box. While he took the ring out of the box, he asked if I would marry him. As he slid the half-carat diamond solitaire on my finger, I said yes. We had picked the ring out together, so it was not a surprise. However, I had no idea how Derek would officially propose to me. Our return to St. Mark's Lighthouse was a beautiful way to propose marriage. Nature was something we both loved. Where better to start our new life together? I kissed him. It was another "Moment in Love." The date was January 16, 1992.

It was time for me to put on the long white gown. I stepped one foot at a time into the skirt of the gown. It was a full gown, laced with shimmering beads at the hem. My arms slipped into the sheer sleeves of the bodice. The sweetheart neckline showed just enough cleavage to be sexy, yet elegant. At five-feet, two inches, I imagined that I was a princess. What a feeling! I knew that only once in a lifetime would I have this moment. I took everything in: the feel of the satin against my skin, the fluffiness of the rented skirt slip underneath, the applying of the make up done so carefully. Everything needed to be perfect. After all, it was MY wedding day! Every princess needs a crown. I was no different. I chose a tiara headpiece with hand-sewn stones that glimmered in the sunlight. My light brown hair sat in soft curls on my shoulders.

The look in my mother's eyes said it all. Her baby was beautiful. She hung the diamond from my father's engagement ring around my neck on a simple gold chain. It was beautiful! It was a reminder that love only last for a moment. My parents had separated when I was thirteen.

The knock at the door signaled that the limousine had arrived. The limousine was a gift from Tony and Vee

Vee. I tried to remember all of the advice that I had given brides over the years as a chauffeur. I couldn't remember a thing. My heart was pounding. I could not believe I was going to be chauffeured in the back of the car I had driven time after time. I was the bride getting married!

The ride to the wedding site went quickly. I tried to rehearse everything in my mind one more time. My first prayer was that there be no rain on my special day. God answered me with a gorgeous day! The sun was shining and there was even a slight breeze despite the forecast of close to ninety degrees. When the limousine stopped at the Eaton Estate, I was met by my hostess who whisked me out of sight into the house. I started asking a million questions. Everybody in the wedding party had arrived on time. The tables and chairs were in place. I really wanted to go outside to look at everything. I wanted to take it all in. Tradition said I couldn't. Before I knew it, it was 5:30 in the evening. One last look in the mirror, my moment had arrived.

Chester, a strong chestnut brown member of the Clydesdale horse family, honored me by pulling my chariot around the lake. His owner, Dave, dressed like a gentleman from the 1800's. As I walked out to the carriage, he tipped his top hat as a salute to not only me, but to my moment. As Dave helped me into the carriage, I felt like one of the royal family in England. I had watched Princess Diana marry Prince Charles on television. Today, I was the Princess! My stepfather, Donald, sat next to me in the carriage. Across from me were Jerome, my ring bearer, the twins as my flower girls, and their younger sister as my trainbearer. (Princess Diana had several trainbearers. Why couldn't I have one?)

The carriage hid behind a row of trees. No one, including my mother, knew about my grand entrance. It was a surprise. I watched the processional through the trees. Our parents lit the lanterns on the gazebo as unity candles, while my friend Carmen Cummings sang, "A Mother's Love." A recording of "Piano in the Dark" played while my bridesmaids walked to the gazebo wearing fuchsia pink tea length dresses. The groomsmen stood on the gazebo like all men do...just looking like they were scared to death of the whole marriage thing! I was taking everything in. I watched as the sun seemed to usher in the wedding party and seem to obey the order of the wedding ceremony by setting ever so slowly in the background. Heaven held back the wind so that my hair would not be blown out of place. The ducks in the pond glided across the water as if they, too were a part of the processional. Everything was perfect!

Chester startled me when he started moving. Dave knew his cue. The "Brazilian Wedding Song" by Quincy Jones seemed to compliment Chester's trot along the edge of the lake. The guest oohed and ahhed. My surprise had worked. The kids were excited about Chester pulling the carriage; so was I. It was a beautiful moment. Chester trotted slowly around the edge of the lake to the rhythm in the song. I did not want this moment to end. I felt tears swell in my eyes. This was MY wedding day. I was marrying the man that I loved.

When Chester stopped at the bridge, my heart started beating incredibly fast. Everyone on the peninsula stood as the song "Moments in Love" started. The kids were helped out of the carriage first. The ring bearer walked across the bridge on cue. Marisha and Marika (the twins) followed. Finally, it was my turn. Dave and Donald helped me out of the carriage. I hadn't realized it was so high. Maybe it was my nerves, but I wanted Chester to be perfectly still while I was exiting the carriage. My trainbearer Terisia was close behind.

I walked slowly across the bridge to the gazebo. The cameras were flashing. I was happy! At that moment, I knew what love felt like. I looked at Derek. He was smiling. That was MY husband on the gazebo waiting for HIS bride. I could not wait to say I do. I do love you with all of my heart and soul. I love you with everything that I can give. I love you unconditionally. I love you!...at least for the moment.

Derek held my hands as we started taking the vows. His hands were strong. They comforted me. They reassured me of his love. Tears of joy streamed down my cheeks. My voice trembled as I vowed my love to Derek. I blocked out the guests. I gazed into Derek's eyes for the entire ceremony. He gazed back. Oh, how great love felt. When the preacher was not looking, Derek mouthed the words I love you. I squeezed his hands. My heart was his. The ceremony passed too quickly. The rings were exchanged. As we knelt, the Lord's Prayer was sung. The time came to pronounce us husband and wife. The passion in Derek's kiss said that he was sharing in this love with me. The ceremony was over in just moments.

We exited the gazebo, kissed our parents, then crossed over the bridge where Chester awaited. Derek sat next to me in the carriage as we pulled away from the bridge. While Chester trotted along the edge of the lake, we kissed. We held each other's hands. We whispered sweet nothings. It was everything that I had dreamed of...at least for the moment.

I could not believe the day had gone so perfectly. A swift jerk caused Chester to break his harness. The guests feared the carriage was going to roll into the lake. The groomsmen ran over to the carriage. Before I knew it, they had swept me out of the carriage, placing me into Derek's strong arms. I was being carried, dress, train, flowers and all, to level ground. I heard someone yell, "Don't drop her!" The laughter rang out from the guests. Another kiss sealed the moment. Everyone applauded. We had just begun the rest of our lives. Nothing could have ruined our moment in love.

The picture taking was done with smooth jazz playing in the background. The guests moved to an area of the lake set up for the reception. A ten-foot high, white, heart shaped balloon arch that was set up on the edge of the lake served as the backdrop for the wedding party's table. Small lanterns adorned with ribbons were the centerpieces. The music played. The flames from the lanterns danced as the sun set ever so slowly. The moments passed.

The first dance snuck up on us quickly. A compact disc of Luther Vandross serenaded us with his wedding song, "Here and Now". Derek held me close and tight. We whispered in each other's ears. He described how his heart started beating when he saw me in the carriage. He told me that I was beautiful. I smiled. I told him how handsome he was. We kissed. The dance ended too quickly. The sun was setting perfectly. The reflection of the orange sunset on the lake was magnificent. The music played softly in the background. The moments were passing.

The traditional tossing of the bouquet was done. A few more pictures were taken. The garter belt was tossed. A few more pictures clicked. The moment had come to have our chauffeur drive us off into the night. The ceremony and reception lasted for over three hours. I didn't want the night to end. It seemed like the time flew too fast. It seemed like just moments ago that I was waking up on my wedding day. I replayed the whole day back in my mind in the limousine. "Moments in Love" was more than a theme, it would become reality.

Apply the lesson in this chapter to your life:

What moment in love am I holding on to?

_____

_____

_____

_____

Do I know what real love is?

_____

_____

_____

_____

Who do I love and why?

_____

_____

_____

_____

Am I willing to pay the price for love?

_____

_____

_____

_____

EVERYTHING HAS A PRICE

CHAPTER EIGHT

BE CAREFUL WHAT YOU ASK FOR...

I am a firm believer that your words, combined with your thoughts, can predict your future. Derek's words predicted a bleak future for our relationship before we ever said, "I DO." Words combined with actions warned me repeatedly that Derek was not the right man for me. Derek should have been careful what he asked for over the years.

As an adjunct professor of speech, I stand behind the podium warning my students that words have powerful consequences. Words can cut to the core of your heart. They can deliver a blow harder than any fist. They can leave wounds so deep that they never completely heal. Words can serve as caution signs that our relationships are in trouble. I should have listened to Derek because his words were the first of many warning signs.

Warning: College

We met when I was eighteen years old. Derek was twenty-three. We were both sophomores in college. Three and a half years later, I was starting law school while he was still working on his bachelor's degree. Year after year, he would make excuses for his lack of motivation. He was working too many hours. His parents tried to help him out by sending him a monthly allotment to ease his load. Derek's parents were wonderful spotters. They wanted him to succeed and so did I. However, he was caught up in a self-pity party. He was caught up in low self-esteem.

He would take a full load of classes, then fail or drop the majority of them. I would be furious. I knew he could do better. I was at a loss. How could he go to class everyday and not pass? He was an intelligent man. He was lying to me. He wasn't going to class. He wasn't studying. He wasn't trying. The problem, in a nutshell, was that HE was not willing to do anything about his situation. Derek had over ten years invested in college, with only three classes remaining to complete his bachelor's degree. I made up excuses for him to his parents and to my friends. I ignored the sign.

Derek did not talk about success. He did not talk about what he would do when he graduated. It was always just one day at a time. I can't recall him ever predicting his graduation from college. I can't recall him ever talking about where he would work when he received his degree. He did not speak it; therefore he never got it. When I tried to have a conversation about his education with him, his response was always that we would take it one day at a time. Another common phrase that he liked to use frequently was, "We'll see." At some point, you have to stop trying and just do. Do in your mind and do with your words. Derek did neither. This was a warning sign. I ignored it.

Warning: Derek keeps leaving

It should have been evident that there was a problem when Derek would not come home for weeks after we argued. During this time, I would fret over how to pay the bills. I would cry while begging him to come back home. I would try to keep people at Taltran out of our business. I would pretend everything was all right. Inside, I was dying. Each time he would leave, we would dig ourselves a bigger hole. He would not pay any of the bills.

I would charge them or deplete our savings.

During my second year in law school, Derek took the car that we were sharing while I was in the middle of final exams. I woke up to find him and the car gone. I panicked. Thank God for spotters because my friends all pitched in to get me back and forth to school for the remainder of the exam week. I didn't know whether I had enough strength or energy to complete the four-hour long exams. My spotters stepped in with words of encouragement, in addition to unbelievable support. One thing was clear in law school, if I did not survive I was not going to succeed. Derek's disregard for not only my future, but *our* future was a sign. I ignored the sign.

I remember clearly going to the bus terminal to talk to Derek about my transportation problem. His response was simple, "I don't care, it is not my problem." He had nothing else to say about the matter. I remember crying and telling him I could not fail any of my exams. His response was chilling: "I said, I don't care! Now get off the bus before I call a supervisor!" When Derek was mad, the look in his eyes could cut the air. He was cold. His heart became hard. I would often tell him he was evil. I did not know anyone who could just turn off their emotions like he could. I had never been in a relationship with someone who, after a few days, didn't call to just check on me. His actions spoke just as loud as his words. I continued to ignore both.

Warning: The hospital

On one occasion, Derek had left for about two weeks. I knew he was staying at a friend's house so, as usual, I went to plead for him to come back. I went over after dark. We talked, I cried. Derek said he did not want to come home. He was not happy. I talked about how we could make it better if he would just give us a chance. I tried positive reinforcement. I understood we had some problems, but they could be worked out. I told him I loved him. I remembered our wedding day. I thought of the moments in love we had shared. Derek interrupted my reflection. He looked me dead in the eye while telling me that he did not love me anymore. I cried harder. We were standing outside of his friend's apartment. He asked me to leave. I did not want to leave without him.

He raised his voice. I raised mine. A few people passing by looked at us as we argued. Derek told me that he did not want me anymore. He did not care about me anymore. He was not in love with me anymore. I felt like he was stabbing me in the heart with each word. Before I knew it, I was sick. Mentally as well as physically. I was crying so hard that I could barely breathe. I yelled at him, asking him why he was doing this to me. His response? "I am not doing anything to you...you are doing it to yourself." I had never felt my chest hurt like that before. I asked Derek for help. He told me to leave. I started hyperventilating. He just stared. I began to vomit in the grass. He did nothing to help me. In fact, he went into the apartment.

I did not know what to do. I did not know what was happening to me. I knew I could not drive. I could barely breathe. I knocked on the door of the apartment. I asked Derek if he could take me to the hospital...something was wrong with me. He told me, "Hell, no." He said that I should not have brought my stupid ass over there in the first place. He did not understand. I needed to go to the hospital! He slammed the door in my face. His friend came outside to check on me. I was sitting down, trying to catch my breath. I told him I needed to go to the hospital. His friend did not have a car. He went inside to ask Derek if he could drive me in our car. Derek said no. He did not care what happened to me. It was my fault. I asked his friend to call a taxi for me. I had no health insurance. There was no way I could afford an ambulance. I sat on the curb of the apartments at almost midnight, waiting for the cab. I saw his friend watching me from the window.

The cab arrived within a few minutes. The driver looked at me with concern. I asked him to please hurry. I was in a great deal of pain. He cracked the windows so that I could get some fresh air. Once I was at the hospital, I was rushed into a room.

Chest pains were serious business. I was hooked up to different machines. One was to determine if I was having heart problems. I was. My heart had been broken! There was not one emergency room doctor who could fix it. The medical prognosis took hours. I kept hoping that Derek would walk into the hospital room. I was too embarrassed to call a friend. I was alone and scared. I fell asleep while the nurse ran tests.

At five in the morning, I was released. I had a chest cold that ended up becoming an infection. That is why it hurt so bad to breathe. The stress of my argument with Derek had sent me into a panic attack, which threw everything off-kilter. My body was reacting to my heartache. The doctor sent me home with two or three prescriptions. I was instructed to go to the campus health clinic in a week for a check up. I had the nurse summon a cab to take me home.

There were no messages on the answering machine when I got home. I was too tired to make it up the stairs. I fell asleep on the sofa. I woke up about eight hours later. I kept waiting for the phone to ring. Didn't Derek care about me? I had no car. My whole body was sore. My head was pounding. I was alone. Why didn't Derek call? It had been over seventeen hours since I left the apartment to go to the hospital. Surely, he had to be concerned. When the phone finally rang, it was close to six that evening. It was Derek.

I was happy to hear from him. However, he was only calling to tell me he would bring me the car. He was not coming home. He also made it clear that he would not come inside when he dropped the car off. Oh, he did ask how I was doing, at the end of the conversation. I said, "Fine." Derek closed the conversation with a simple, "I told you not to come over here. I don't know when you will start listening to me." It would take years before I heard what he was saying.

As the years passed, our moments in love were few and far between. There were no phone calls just to say hello. There were no romantic dinners. There was barely any sex. Derek slept in another room or on the floor most of the time. The dynamics of our relationship had completely changed. I wanted more than survival. I wanted to succeed. I wanted to work on our relationship. He had given up years ago. I wanted a nice house. He could care less if we lived in a shack. Derek would tell me these things. I wanted to be his friend. He didn't need me as his friend. He was trying to warn me. I ignored him.

Warning: The house
We moved to Orlando after college. It was a rough transition. I left him in Tallahassee with the understanding that he might not move with me. A few months later, he got a job offer in Orlando. We were together again. We lived in a townhouse for three years. I wanted a house. Derek said okay, but all he was going to do for me was get me in it.

When we were looking at homes, Derek would always warn me to find a home that I could afford on my salary. He would remind me that if he left, I would be responsible for the mortgage...so, I had better get one that I could afford. That was a big red flag. I ignored it.

Warning: The job
Another flag should have gotten my attention. He had a great opportunity to change careers. He sabotaged it. I

could not understand him. He complained about his current job, yet would not do anything about it. A perfect job opportunity presented itself. He did not take advantage of it! The agency wanted Derek. They processed his application quickly, set up an interview, and then, he blew it! He didn't study the practice questions for the exam. He passed the exam by just a point or two. There was a physical required, but he didn't run or do any physical training. He passed the physical, despite his lack of effort. A psychological review was required. He purposely gave information that he knew would reflect negatively on his hiring status. He said that our marriage was more down than it was up. No, really? I wonder why.

I was pissed! I had done nothing but support him through years of complete hell. But as I laid in bed that night, I knew I could not blame Derek for my anger. I was angry because I had let the situation get to this point. I had hoped. I had believed. I had prayed for a change. However, Derek did not want a change. He would say he did not care whether he got the job or not. He would say he was not worried about it. His words predicted his not getting the job. I ignored the caution sign.

I loved him! I wanted him to love me back. I was living in that moment of love that had taken place years before. I was not blameless in this situation. I did my share of yelling, name calling, and cursing. This was not about blame. It was about consequences for our words and actions. Over the years, I nagged and complained. I did not create the best home environment. I admit that. I brought up his laziness and weak spots during arguments. I felt the sting of his words. I am sure he felt the sting of mine.

Derek would ask for space when he left. I did not know what he meant by "space." He could not explain it to me. He just knew he was not happy. I thought space meant he wanted to see someone else, or perhaps he would never come back. I was afraid to let go. I didn't want to lose him. I never said the words, "I don't love you." I never told him that I did not want him. I loved him with all of my heart. I believed in our vows. I believed it could work. I always wanted to talk about it. He said he could not talk to me. His take on it was that I talked too much. I was caught up. Derek wanted to be released.

As the years passed, the words got harsher. The words were powerful. I don't believe that Derek realized what his words were going to cost him. I don't believe he knew what he was asking for. The statements had a price, just like the questions. They stuck in my mind:

I don't want you anymore...I told you that a long time ago!

I don't care where I live...I can stay in my truck...as long as you are not there!

You need to find a boyfriend...you are too much to maintain!

Ask your girlfriends to go with you...I don't want to go!

Don't tell me about your work...I don't want to hear it!

I told you that I don't love you.

I have never been in love with you.

I made a mistake.

You are a lazy f--k!

You are a lazy b--ch!

I hate you!

If you don't like it...why don't you do something about it?

The warning signs kept flashing throughout the years. By the time I acknowledged the red light, I was in the middle of the road trying to put on the brakes. I prayed that I would not be killed in a head-on collision because I had run so many lights before. Derek had asked the right question: *"What was I going to do about it?"*

Apply the lessons in this chapter to your life:

What have you asked for?

_____

_____

_____

_____

Once you received it, was it really what you wanted?

_____

_____

_____

_____

What things do you regret asking for?

_____

_____

_____

What are the things you should be asking for and haven't?

_____

_____

_____

_____

CHAPTER NINE

WHAT ARE YOU GOING TO DO ABOUT IT?

My first assignment at the State Attorney's Office was in the traffic division. I dealt primarily with DUI's and reckless driving charges for the eight months that I was in that unit. My first judge was a young, black man by the name of Reginald K. Whitehead. I really respected Judge Whitehead, for many reasons. The one thing that sticks out in my mind about Judge Whitehead was that he always said the following words at the end of a sentencing, hearing, or court proceeding: "Good luck to you, sir or ma'am." There is one case that deserves special attention.

It was a Friday morning; we had completed all of the cases on the docket. In the back of the courtroom were a woman and her husband. We, meaning the judge, the court deputies, and myself, were preparing to leave the courtroom when I noticed them. The woman had long red hair that flowed down her thin, short body. The man was clean cut with a tall slender build. It was the woman that moved me. She approached me with tears swelling in her eyes. The husband stood silent. "Ma'am, can you help us?" she asked me in a soft voice. As an instructor of communications, I know that nonverbal communication can say more than words on any given day. Today was one of those days.

The woman, through tears, explained that her

lawyer was not there. She had called his office to find out where he was. She was told that he was out sick today. Her husband was facing his third DUI. They knew he was going to jail. They had prepared themselves, along with their three kids, that today was going to be the day that daddy was going to jail. I guessed that the tears were coming because what they had prepared themselves for was now being delayed. We have a policy in our office that we do not talk to defendants. There are many reasons for this; the main one being that defendants have constitutional rights. You always see police officers on television tell a suspect that he/she has the right to remain silent, anything they say can be used against them in a court of law. The same holds true when talking to a prosecutor.

I explained to the wife that I could not speak to her husband. I suggested they talk with their lawyer. The lawyer would reset the court date. At that time, the judge would sentence her husband accordingly. The woman really broke down at that point. She started telling me that just the day before, the attorney's secretary had called them to make sure they were making the final payment.

They had given the attorney the last bit of money they had. She could not understand how the attorney could call for money, but not notify them that he was not going to be in court today. (The attorney had not called the judge's office, either.) Of course, I had no answers for why the attorney had done what he did. But I felt this woman's pain. By this time, the husband had tears in his eyes. He was sitting on a nearby bench. The wife told me that there had been a warrant out for her husband. He had contemplated running. He had thought of just leaving her and the kids with a note. She begged him to talk with their pastor while trying to assure him that everything was going to be okay.

This woman seemed to have incredible strength. I listened to her as she shared with me how she had sat her husband down to tell him this was his fault. He knew better, and now he was going to have to face his wrong doings. The pastor had said the same thing, after listening to the story. But the pastor went one step further. That same afternoon, the pastor called me to tell me that the husband had come to him to tell him about the warrant. The pastor's response was somewhat harsh. "Son, you went out there, got drunk, and drove. That was simple for you, right?" The husband responded, "Yes, sir." The preacher continued, "So, now you have a warrant out for your arrest. You can run, wait for them to pick you up at home or at your job, or you can take responsibility and turn yourself in and serve your time. Those are the options...now, here is the question. '*What are you going to do about it?*'"

I was listening to this Southern Baptist minister on the phone. I could picture him saying every word. The preacher told me, "Ma'am, I believe in calling it like I see it. I don't play with my members and pretend that God will solve everything for them. Especially, when God did not put them in the situation." I wanted to say, "Amen, pastor!" (This is what I have been preaching for years!) However, I did not dare to interrupt him. I could tell he was older, probably close to sixty. It was clear that he meant business. He continued, "I try to teach the doctrine of self help. You can make things what they are. I tell my members, don't come to me complaining about a job situation or low pay if you haven't taken any steps to do something about it." Most ministers who came to court for their members, came with a sob story. He's a good man, in church every Sunday, hard worker, yada yada yada. But not this preacher! He was calling me to ask me when the man could go to jail! I was shocked!

I explained that his attorney would be responsible for resetting the hearing. In closing, the preacher said, "I did not tell him what to do. I gave him the options. It was his choice. He decided to turn himself in and serve the time."

The hearing was reset for the following week. The man returned with his wife. The pastor was also present. The judge asked the man if he had anything to say before sentencing. The man said, "Your honor, I was wrong. My pastor helped me to see that. I probably knew it from the start. But, I want to make things right. I want to serve my time. I want to set an example for my boys. I sat down with them to explain that Daddy was wrong. Daddy could have hurt somebody. So now, Daddy has to serve time to pay for what he did. Your honor, I accept my responsibility. I understand I must go to jail." You don't hear that very often in my job!

The wife was sobbing quietly behind him. The pastor was holding her. I think everyone in the courtroom was touched by his words. I asked the judge to consider the work release program, but I stood firm on the jail sentence. The judge sentenced him to jail. But he was allowed to serve the time in the work release program. This program allowed his family to continue to receive the income from his employer. He was permitted to keep his job. However, he spent each night in jail. The judge also lengthened the sentence by a few months, since it was not straight jail time. Judge Whitehead closed as the man was being handcuffed, "Good luck to you, sir."

The wife gave me a hug. She said, "Thank you for taking the time to listen to me last Friday. I appreciate your recommending work release. I am glad you were our prosecutor." You don't hear that very often, either. The pastor also shook my hand and said, "See how the Lord took care of him once he decided that he was going to do the right thing?" I understood exactly what the preacher meant. The man, despite going to jail, was going to keep his job. Most importantly, his family was going to be provided for. The outcome probably would have been much different if he had not turned himself in.

There have been so many times that I have had to ask myself, "Veraunda, what are you going to do about it?" I can recall talking to friends about situations. In my mind, I would know that until I decided what to do about it and DID IT, I would be stuck in the same situation.

'Don't get caught up' is the first big step we should take to prevent heartache down the road. Reality says it is not always possible to avoid getting caught up. Our emotions start to control us in certain situations. We lose the ability to stop at the caution signs. As a result, we find ourselves in difficult situations. We complain. We moan. We seek advice from others. But the bottom line is that until we decide what *we are going to do about it,* the situation will remain the same. This has been an extremely difficult lesson for me to learn.

My marriage was deteriorating fast. It had taken six years of challenges before I realized I had to DO SOMETHING ABOUT IT...for me! This is a key point. *I had to do something for me!* Not for Derek...because I could not change Derek. I could not come up with an answer for Derek. I had to focus all of my energy inward. I had gotten caught up in the golden "moment of love." I had bench-pressed all I could, time after time. I had prayed, tried counseling, and cut back on my involvement in the community. I had tried all I knew. I had been a passenger on the bus. When I got on the bus, my destination was love. Somewhere, the bus took a wrong turn. I watched the situation spin out of control. I forgot how to ring the bell. I didn't know when to ring the bell. I wasn't even sure where to get off the bus. I didn't know where my stop was.

I let my desire to honor my wedding vows cost me my happiness. I let my fear of what people would say cost me my peace. I let fear of financial disaster cost me my independence. I let my childhood experience with my parent's divorce overshadow my freedom. Love almost cost me my life!

Our sixth wedding anniversary should have been a happy one. We had just bought a house. We celebrated the purchase of our home in connection with our wedding anniversary. I surprised Derek with a two-night stay at the Walt Disney World Contemporary Resort. It is a famous resort pictured on post cards because the monorail travels through the middle of the resort. On our very first trip to Disney five years before, he mentioned how he had always wanted to stay in the Contemporary Resort. I loved to surprise him. If he wanted it, and I could afford it, he got it.

The resort was very nice. However, something was missing. There was no affection. There was no handholding while walking through the park. There were no sweet little nothings being whispered. There were no kisses. We had sex, but there was no intimacy. Over the three days that we spent celebrating our wedding anniversary, Derek never told me he loved me. My mind started to process the information I had been receiving for the past six years. The constant verbal abuse and the threats of divorce were playing in my head. He did not want to be in this marriage.

On more than one occasion we would be in the heat of an argument when Derek would look me dead in the eye and state the following words: "If you don't like it, do something about it." Those words echoed in my head the entire drive home from the resort. The date was May 31st, 1998. I will never forget it because it was the day I made up my mind that *I was going to do something about it.*

Derek had threatened me with a divorce within six months of our wedding. The threats never stopped. Every argument was solved with his declaring we could just get a divorce. I was ready to do something about MY situation. He had talked about a divorce year after year. I was ready to give him what he asked for!

July 16th was the final warning sign. I was packing to go visit a friend in Seattle. I had told Derek that I wanted a divorce. I was tired. I was tired of fighting. I was tired of trying to support him emotionally. I was tired of the lack of romance. I was tired of wondering where he was. I was tired of being tired. Most important, I was tired of trying. I did not have the strength to just survive from one anniversary to the next. It was clear this marriage was costing much more than it was worth. I had no idea it was almost to cost me my life.

As a lawyer, I knew we needed a plan. I approached Derek on this Saturday evening to discuss how we would divide up the bills. Things had been extremely rough for the past two months. I tried to tread lightly. It didn't work. Our voices started rising. Name-calling followed. It was ugly, to say the least. I gave Derek two weeks to get out of the house. I wanted a civil divorce. This was going to be hard, but I had to do something about my life. Enough was enough. I did not need him anymore. I did not want him anymore. I was not *in love* with him anymore. I learned from the best. Derek was my teacher.

I huffed downstairs to the master bedroom. Before I knew what hit me, Derek ran down the stairs, picked me up, and threw me on the bed. He started punching the wooden headboard. I was lying flat on my back. Derek's 280 pound muscular frame was on top of me. My hands were bound by one of his large hands. He used the other to destroy the headboard with vicious blows. There were candles on the headboard to soothe my spirit in the evenings. As Derek delivered the blows, the glass from the candelabras shattered. I was terrified. We had never been at this juncture before.

I cried hysterically. I begged Derek to let me go. I would leave. I would get my stuff. I would just go. He could have the house. I would go live with one of my parents. Derek got angrier the more I talked. I begged to use the phone. I needed help. This situation was beyond my control. Derek pulled the phone out of the wall.

The language was harsh; the grip on my hands was painful. "Derek, you are hurting me!" I screamed. His response was, "I don't care. I will kill you, bitch!" All I could say in my mind was...Oh, my God!

Derek's knees were straddling me on the bed. I could not move. I didn't try. I saw Derek grab a large piece of glass from the crushed headboard. I heard him saying I would be taken out of the house in a body bag. When I felt him press the sharp edge of the glass up against my neck, it was more than I could take. I begged for his mercy. Derek told me to shut up. My mind raced back before I could stop it.

I was back on the ground downtown, behind the building with rocks against my back; pleading for my life. For the second time in my life, I was on my back with a man on top of me. I was begging for my life. This time, it was the man I had loved that was raping me. He was raping me of my dignity. He never entered me physically. It wasn't the thrust of his body that was chilling. It was the thrust of his words. It was the look on his face. At that moment, I knew he was capable of killing of me. The pain from a piece of shattered glass on the bed scratching my arm brought me back to reality.

There is no way to describe what goes on in your mind when you believe you are about to die. Your mind operates at tremendous speeds. You think about everything simultaneously. I thought about the fact that I was a prosecutor who had represented women in domestic violence cases. I thought about all the reports I had read of women whose lives were almost taken at the hands of their lovers. I thought about the pictures I had seen of blood and bruises. I recalled the injuries inflicted upon women who thought they were in love. I remembered the stern lecturing I gave repeatedly to women who chose to stay with their abusers. I remembered telling them *they had to do something about it!*

I tried to focus my mind. I could not help thinking that my fancy gold law enforcement badge, inscribed with the words Assistant State Attorney, had no power now. It was a gruesome reality; my position as a prosecutor was just that...a position. I fought for justice everyday for others. Now, I was fighting for my life. I felt powerless. Derek had the power to end my life. He was in control of whether I would live or die. I did the only thing I knew how to do. I prayed. GOD, PLEASE HELP ME!

I felt the glass pressing against my neck; my arms were hurting from being held over my head. I had to stay calm. I had to think. There was one thing I was sure of...if I survived this one, it was over! The "moment in love" was over!

I asked Derek if I could go to the bathroom. He said no. I told him I had to go really badly. "No, just go on the bed," he said. I asked a third time. He accompanied me to the master bathroom. This wasn't going to work. I thought if I could get in the bathroom, I could escape. The windows were large sliding windows. I could knock out the screen, then climb out of the window. My first problem was that the bathroom door was a sliding one with no lock. The second was that Derek would not leave me in the bathroom alone.

Cooperating with the man who raped me downtown had saved my life. I decided that I should try it with Derek. I asked him what he would like me to do. He told me to sit on the floor. I sat. He said, "You wanted to talk earlier, so talk now." I did not have anything to say. This made him angrier. It was a rage within him that I had never seen before. I really didn't know what to say, but it was clear that I better think of something. I could only go back to our wedding day. I sobbed softly while remembering our "moments in love." I asked Derek if he remembered holding my hand in the gazebo while we took our vows. He did not answer. I asked him if he remembered telling me he loved me as I cried during the ceremony. He seemed to be remembering. He shook his head from left to right as if he was pondering what had happened. My next sentence was simple, but powerful. With the softest tone I could muster I said, "Derek, you know if there was any hope for us before tonight...it is over now." His response was just as simple, "Yes." The rage was gone. The reality had hit us both. There was no turning back.

I continued to sit on the floor, speaking in a soft voice to Derek. *"Derek, you know that I really loved you. I did everything I could to make our marriage work. You asked for this divorce time after time. You told me you didn't want me, over and over again. You told me you didn't love me. You asked me what I was going to do about it. In fact, you challenged me to do something about it. I am prepared to take care of myself. I deserve to be happy. I deserve to be loved."*

Derek began to cry. I felt sorry for him. I didn't want to hurt him, just to free him. More importantly, to free myself. I told him he needed to call a friend to make arrangements for the next couple of days. The prosecutor in me said, *"You know, Derek, if I called the police on you, you would be facing some serious charges...False imprisonment, aggravated battery with a deadly weapon, not to mention attempted murder. I love you enough to know that if I called the police, you would go to prison for a substantial amount of time. It would ruin your life. So my suggestion to you is, don't make this hard for me. Leave, because I don't want to see you in prison. I don't want to have to testify against you. I don't want the embarrassment or the publicity. I just want to be free."*

Derek called one of his friends to come over. The friend arrived within a short period of time with his wife. The wife tried to talk to me. I didn't want to talk. She was trying to convince me that my marriage could be saved. She had no idea the price I had paid for the past ten years. I didn't have the energy to tell her. Derek packed a bag, then left. That night, I sat in our new home and cried. A sense of fear came over me when I realized I had almost lost my life.

I left for Seattle four days later, to just get away. I had to pull myself together. I had to reflect, regroup, and renew my inner strength. Seattle is beautiful. The mountains seem to roll into the bay. I hiked Mt. Ranier with my best friend, Jaydee. We went shopping in the malls. We visited the famous Pike's Market. It felt so good to be free.

As we ate dinner on the bay one night, a young couple was getting married on a yacht in the bay. The sun was setting so beautifully. The backdrop of the mountains was majestic. The bride looked beautiful in her white gown. Her pictures would be perfect. She could not have asked for a better day. I prayed that her "moment in love" would last longer than mine had. I thought about how perfect my wedding day had been. I questioned why it ended so violently. As I watched the wedding party on the yacht, a nice breeze blew threw my hair. I didn't want to go home.

A week later, the process started for me to finalize what I was going to do about my marriage. I needed to finish what I had started. Getting Derek out of my life meant work. I traded in my car to get his name off of my old one. I got my banking accounts in order. I closed some credit accounts. I took his name off of others. I called my creditors to tell them it might be a little rough for a while. I asked for their patience. The process had begun. Derek and I set up a payment schedule. I did not trust him with paying the bills directly. I had been the bookkeeper in the relationship for the past ten years. I would remain in the house. Derek would pay his half of the credit card debt.

I would be responsible for all bills associated with the house.

I was certain I would survive. I knew it would be rough, but I had no idea how rough. Derek promised to make my life hell when he left. He promised the divorce would be a nasty one. He told me he had spoken with a lawyer. He would be the one filing for the divorce. I was fine with that. The problem was that after two months; Derek stopped paying his part of the bills. I received a letter from his lawyer indicating he wanted the papers to the house prior to resuming any payments. I refused.

There was no way I was going to give up anything more than I already had. For years, I thought about what other people would think. For years, I stressed myself over what was best for Derek. Not anymore! I had played these games for years. I was going to make the rules this time. I did not know a lot about family law. I did not have enough money to hire a lawyer. So, I did the best I knew how. I drafted a letter to the attorney with the help of some lawyer friends. (None of my friends really practiced family law, either.) The letter detailed my desires for the dissolution of marriage settlement. I wanted Derek to be responsible for the credit card debt he had created. This letter was sent in October.

Derek kept his promise to make my life a living hell. He refused to pay a dime. It was his way of controlling me, or so he thought. He talked about me like a dog to my friends and family. It hurt, but it was okay. I was surviving. Each month, I called my creditors to explain when they would get their payment. I worked overtime teaching extra classes at the police academy while taking on an additional speech class at the community college. Financially, I was devastated. My student loans were close to being sent to a collection agency.

I received a phone call from Derek in December. His tone was evil. I was directed not to call him at work about the bills. I was directed not to speak to his parents. He wanted to know when I was filing for a divorce. I told him I wasn't. I could not afford to because I was paying for his bills. He had a lawyer. He could do it. He told me that if I didn't file by my birthday in January, he was going to file. That was what I wanted him to do. I should have known he wasn't going to DO anything.

I was still paying the price for our "moments in love." I was paying bills for "our" dreams. The stress of surviving was costing me emotionally. The physical demands of my work schedule were grueling. I had been down this road before. I knew the bottom line was that if I could muster up the strength to succeed, I had the potential to survive. Surviving meant being willing to pay the price by getting off my butt to file the paperwork. I had become complacent. I had forgotten that I was the one saying I was ready to DO something about my situation.

Seven months later, Derek had not filed for divorce. Why was I waiting on Derek to do something about MY situation? I was the one who said I was fed up. I swallowed my pride. I accepted a two hundred dollar loan from one of my spotters, Veronica, to file for the divorce. I had let seven months go by without holding Derek responsible. I could hear him challenging me to do something about it. On March 15th, 1999, I did it. I filed the divorce papers with the Clerk of the Court in Orange County, Florida.

It should have been a simple process. Mediation is mandatory in Orange County for divorces in which there is no settlement agreement. The mediation could be set within a matter of weeks, once Derek was served with the papers. Derek was not going to make this easy. The sheriff's deputy went to serve Derek with the divorce papers on March 16th at his place of employment. I had no idea where Derek was living. I had no choice but to provide his work address on the court paperwork.

Derek played games by dodging service for over a month. The server would go to his job an hour before he was to arrive. Derek would call in sick. The server called his employer to request a home address. Derek had not changed his address from my home address. He did not change his driver's license as required by law.

After so many tries, the sheriff returns the paperwork to the court. The next step is to place an advertisement in the newspaper. If there is no response to the newspaper ad, the divorce is considered uncontested. I would get what I asked for by default. The server explained this to Derek's supervisor on her last attempt to serve him. Two days later, Derek went to the sheriff's office to sign for the papers.

On May 6th, I got a phone call from my father; my only brother had died. (My parents only had my brother and I.) I was in the middle of a child abuse trial. I was devastated. The day could not get any worse. Wrong! While I was waiting for the jury to come back with a verdict, my mother joined me at the courthouse. She accompanied me to the clerk's office to see if Derek had filed a response to the petition for divorce. So, on the day of my brother's death, I learned Derek wanted me to pay for almost everything, including his lawyer and health insurance. I was furious!

My emotions ran from grieving to disbelief. My mother reassured me I would survive. I knew she was right. I needed to get my family through my brother's funeral. I would deal with Derek later. Before we finalized my brother's funeral arrangements, I had called the mediation office to set our case for a hearing. I was tired. I needed closure.

I did not have enough money to hire an attorney, so I was a pro se litigant. I was upset that Derek could afford an attorney. But I knew why. He wasn't paying a dime toward any of his bills. I would have to suck it up. I had to pull myself together. I started this process. It was time.

I was nervous about seeing him after almost a year. We had only talked on the phone three or four times. Derek was angry each time we talked. Most of the conversations would end abruptly, with him hanging up the phone on me. We had not been able to resolve anything by telephone. I was afraid the same might be true with the mediation process. I did not want to have a trial. I stood in front of judges everyday for other people. I was scared to represent myself. I was afraid my emotions would overshadow my legal abilities. I prayed mediation would resolve the matter.

I asked my friend, Helen, to go with me. She was a lawyer who worked with me. She would be my emotional support during the hearing. She had spotted me throughout the process. She had a good head on her shoulders. Derek objected to her being present, which left me alone. I began to cry out of anger and frustration. He had someone to represent him. Yet, he did not want me to have anyone. It was a control issue. I always knew he was evil! Helen reassured me I would be okay. She reminded me to stand my ground. I took a deep breath, then wiped my eyes. I refused to let him see me like this.

Mediation went better than I expected. We had an outstanding mediator. She ran the show completely. She asked what issues were in dispute. The house was the biggest issue, according to both of us. Derek had threatened to make me sell it. He refused to sign it over to me. (This, despite the fact that I had been totally responsible for all of the mortgage and upkeep for the past year.) People can become such jerks in a divorce. You think you know your spouse? Get a divorce. You will discover a whole new person was living with you.

The mediator explained the law, stating that I could ask for half of all the bills for the entire time we were together, including the time we were separated. This included the mortgage and upkeep of the house. The way she saw it, my request for only half of the joint credit card bills was more than reasonable. She also explained that he could not make me sell the house. The judge would probably make him buy me out if he wanted a trial. Things were starting to make sense. He would lose if we went to trial. We came to an agreement within an hour. I was relieved.

As we were waiting on the copies of the agreement, Derek had the nerve to ask me for some of the wedding pictures. Yeah right...we were getting a divorce, why did he need to be reminded of our wedding? They were mine... it was my "moment in love". It was my vision of love. (I had to make at least one major stand...I had given him everything he wanted.) Derek had asked for his name back during one of his last big productions in the house. I was happy to oblige that request. I did not want to take his name in the first place. But, trying to stroke his male ego, I agreed, against my better judgement. Now, he wanted it back? I quickly reminded the mediator that I wanted to restore my maiden name. He could have his name! It never did a thing for me! But, no pictures! He could call the photographer; they still had the negatives!

Getting out of the marriage was harder than getting into it. I waited for months for his lawyer to set a final hearing date. I had to keep calling to find out why Derek's payments were late. This was absolutely ridiculous! After two months of playing a wait-and-see game, I was reminded by a friend that I needed to DO something about it. There was no reason I could not call the judge to set a hearing date. What was I waiting on? Why was I putting my situation in Derek's hands?

The first date I set, no one appeared. I could not believe it. The proper notices were sent to both Derek and his attorney. Would this part of my life ever end? I reset the date for a week later. This time, it was official. Derek accompanied his lawyer to the final hearing. Believe it or not, it was a sad occasion. I looked at him, realizing that this was it. The official end to what had started out as with a fairy tale wedding. It was over. I think both of us were humbled by the realization that it was final. There were no hostile words; no evil looks. I wanted to just sit down with him in a quiet place to talk about what went wrong. How did we get to this place, a courtroom full of people who all wanted a divorce?

The judge called our case within a few moments. I was at work...the courthouse is my place of business. I did not know the judge, which was a relief. The judge asked if our marriage was irretrievably broken. I thought about the question. It had been for quite some time. Derek and I both answered with a simple yes. I was almost embarrassed. Our marriage had not survived. That is what this divorce meant. We had failed! I quickly had to remind myself that I had tried everything I knew. There are times in life when we must let go. This was one of them.

The judge signed the paperwork, restored my maiden name, then sealed the file. It was over. Derek did not say anything, but his face, like mine, showed signs of pain. It was not the joyous occasion I thought it would be. There was no shouting for joy. Instead, I went back to Helen's office and cried.

I knew I did the right thing. I made a decision that I had to follow through to the end. I felt a slight sense of relief that the process had ended. Yet, I wished it had not come to this point. I was torn. On one hand, I watched for years as my moments in love dwindled. On the other, I wanted just one more golden moment of love. I wanted something to confirm those moments were not lies. I wanted to go back in time. I wanted to hear the blend of the instruments. I wanted to feel the beat of the melody. I wanted to slip into the white gown. I wanted to dance one more time. I wanted to feel "in love" at least for one more moment.

The reality was that the moment had passed years ago. Zora Neale Hurston's suspicion was right: much that had passed for constant love was just a golded up moment, walking in its sleep. I had woken up from this wonderful dream of love. Somewhere in the middle of the night, my dream had turned into a nightmare. That nightmare ended on August 6th, 1999, almost ten years after our first Moment in Love.

I went to dinner with Jaydee on the evening of the divorce. We talked about all that had gone wrong over the years in my marriage. We talked about how much I had been willing to pay to keep one moment in love. Reflection is a powerful tool for self-growth. I realized I had taken years to accept reality. I had struggled with what people would say, how I would make it, and the fear of failure. In the long run, it took me almost losing my life to see how much I was paying for a moment that had passed.

One of my older and wiser friends, Sandra, told me years before that I would know when I had had enough. When I came to that point, she said I would do something about it. Sandra was right. Just like the preacher told his congregation, there are options once you find yourself in unpleasant situations. The question becomes, "What are you going to do about it?"

How does this chapter apply to my life:

Are you where you want to be?

_____

_____

_____

_____

_____

If not, what are you going to do about it?

_____

_____

_____

_____

_____

EVERYTHING HAS A PRICE

CHAPTER TEN

THE CLOSING ARGUMENT

When I was a sophomore in college, my signature statement was: "The ultimate goal in life is to be happy with yourself." Ladies and gentlemen, you have some decisions to make if you want to be "successful." You are in control of your own destiny. However, the path to your success will have plenty of turns and hurdles. I assure you, if you just stay on the path and keep jumping, the rewards will be great.

We have to learn to start where we are. Discover what situations have you caught up. Probe all areas of your life…your relationships with friends or family, your job, your finances, and your mental health. There may be several areas in need of repair. Remember that personal growth is often accompanied by pain. Anyone can figure out they have problem areas. But it takes courage to create change.

I often think of my life as a house. When I bought my house, I liked it. I was excited about owning my first home. But, from day one, I knew there was a lot of work needed. My real estate agent and I walked through the house envisioning how nice it could be with a little work. The outside, as well as the inside, needed to be repainted. The carpet needed to be replaced. Tile would look really nice in the bathrooms, kitchen and dining room. The yard needed work. The sprinklers did not work properly. The grass looked awful. The backyard didn't have a fence. I think you get the picture...there was much work to be done.

At the time I closed on the house, I was not focusing on all the work that needed to be done. I was so happy about moving into a house that I gladly accepted the challenge of bringing it up to my standards. I knew the house had potential. I was realistic about the costs of this project. I understood that I had a budget. There was no way to do everything I wanted all at once. I prioritized my "To Do List."

I started with the painting and flooring. I had to consider styles. The next step was comparing prices. I spent my weekends shopping for the right tile and carpet. When I found the carpet I liked, I had to charge it. I did not want to get in deeper debt. On the other hand, if I waited to have the carpet installed after I moved in, it would be a huge hassle. I would have to take off from work and move all the furniture around after struggling to get it moved in the house. I decided it was better for me to pay the price for carpet now, instead of suffering the inconvenience later.

The tile was the same scenario...shop, compare, then have it installed. If I waited to have the tile put in later, I would have a mess on my hands. The dust from tearing up the original tile would be everywhere. I would have to clean extensively after the installation. I did not need any extra work, so I decided to have the tile installed prior to moving in the house as well.

The painting was a little easier. My stepfather paints. I took him up on his offer. He saved me a significant amount of money. I gave him a key to the house. He determined his own schedule for painting the week before we moved in. The tile, carpet and paint made a tremendous difference in the appearance of the house. I was pleased.

There was one small problem. The three projects exhausted my budget. I had a list a mile long of "wants." I wanted new window drapery. I wanted knew furniture. I wanted to add a deck onto the back of the house. Reality made it clear, I could only do one thing at a time. My wants would have to wait. Wants cost. Needs cost, also. I did not have enough to cover both. In fact, I did not have enough to pay for all of my needs.

I had taken pictures of the house when we moved in. One afternoon about two months after I had been in the house, I looked through the pictures. Not only was I amazed at the progress, I was pleased with it. The pictures helped me to refocus. I had a vision of what I would like the house to look like when it was completed. Little by little, it was becoming the house I had envisioned.

I did not spend a lot of time on the outside of the house. I spend the majority of my time inside. The outside appearance was important, but people would only be outside for a moment. The real time is spent inside a house. You want the inside to be comfortable. I like to have it all together. When I come home, I like a clean house. I want everything to be in its place. I want to be at peace in my home. I fight the rest of the world the majority of the day. My home should be a haven of rest. I enjoy my home because I have worked hard for it. I walk inside the house knowing it is not where I want it to be…but it isn't where it used to be either. There are times when I have to remind myself, Veraunda, it is a process, be patient.

I looked for houses almost two years before finding one that I knew was right for me. I had to save money for a year before I could afford the closing costs. Each house I looked at had room for improvement. Yes, that includes the new homes. I liked one thing here, or something else there. In the long run, I had to make choices. The bottom line was simple. How much could I afford to pay for what

I wanted? I took it one step further, how could I get the most for my money?

Life is very practical. We are the ones who place value on the things in our life. The exact floor plan of my house sold for $40,000 more in a different neighborhood. I had to be sensible. I did not need to buy a house that would consume my entire paycheck. Common sense told me to work with what I had. Be creative. Envision the house the way you want it to be. Figure out what it will take to remodel it. Then DO IT!

I saved $40,000 up front by buying the pre-owned house instead of the new one. I spent a few dollars remodeling the basics. I saw the progress. Now, I am working on remodeling one room at a time. I have to set a budget for each project. When I run out of money or energy, I take a break from the project. I reflect, regroup, then renew the work.

At times, in the midst of remodeling, the room looks a mess. Things are in disarray. I often think of how horrible the room looks when you take everything out and start remodeling. The dust flies everywhere. The sound of the saws or hammering is agitating. But oh, when the work is complete, the results are wonderful. Not to mention worth the price you paid.

The inconvenience of having to take off from work to meet the contractors fades. The frustration that the work may not have been completed on the date it was promised by the contractor diminishes. The extra money you had to shell out for unforeseen problems is not the issue anymore. The project is finished now. No need to linger in the past. You got what you wanted because you found the strength to survive through the process. All that matters in the end is the result of the labor.

Each area in your life can be labeled as a room in the house. Start by making sure you have a firm foundation for the house. Are you in a solid place with your inner self?

Are you at peace in your home? Do you believe that your house has potential? Does the house need remodeling? Set priorities. Determine a budget. There are two things to consider here. How much can you afford to pay to get your house where you would like for it to be? How much are you willing to pay for the work that needs to be done. This is often a hard question to answer. There have been several occasions where the consequences for not paying to have the work done cost me more in the end. Often, I was not sure I could afford the work. In my personal life, there are times when I am not sure what needs to be done. I know that something is leaking. I just don't know where the leak is coming from.

While I was writing this book, a pipe in a wall sprung a leak. I did not know that was the problem when I found water on the floor in a storage closet. I tried home remedies for two days because I could not find where the water was coming from. Finally, I heard the constant sound of water spraying. I was forced to call in a plumber. He spent several hours trying to find the leak. He started with the obvious places, under the sink, the bathroom fixtures, and the toilet valves. None of them were leaking.

He explained the next step was that he might have to tear up the tile to see if the pipes in the foundation were the cause of the problem. I dreaded this. I had paid good money for the tile. I did not want to see it ruined. I certainly did not want to pay to have it redone. My thoughts were scattered: What if they don't have the pattern I chose anymore? What if the dust from tearing the tile ruins my belongings? How much is this going to cost? The plumber promised me he would do everything he could to make the repair with minimum cost or damage.

I knew the work had to be done. The consequence for not repairing the problem was major flooding in my home. I was relieved when he found the pipe that was leaking in a bedroom closet. He had to cut the wall to get to the pipe. I did not like the idea, but the wall would be minor to repair compared to trying to clean up after a flood. Once he found the pipe, it still took quite a while to repair it. He had to get inside the wall, turn the water off, fix the pipe, and clean up the mess where the leak had occurred. And, of course, I had a nice little bill at the conclusion of the repair.

Was it worth it? Absolutely! The work had to be done. I did not anticipate a pipe breaking when I bought my house. I did not put emergency repairs in my budget. I did not have any extra money set aside for this situation. However, I sacrificed. I found the money. I was not happy about shelling out a few hundred dollars for a pipe. But I understood that I wanted a house. When I bought the house, I knew I would have to maintain it. I knew that I would have to repair items along the way. If I wanted to keep the house in good condition, it meant paying the price to repair things as they came up. If you don't repair things when you first discover the problem, they usually get worse. This means that fixing the problem becomes more expensive because there is more damage.

One project at a time, make your vision become a reality. Start with the problem area that is causing you the most pain or damage. There may be some things you have to totally remodel or repair. Perhaps you want to go back to school, change careers, or start a family. Take it one room at a time. Don't try to overhaul your life all at once. It will be an overwhelming job. You'll become frustrated and quit. So, start where you are. Map out a plan for your project. Expect some delays. Count on some detours. Be patient and be realistic.

Ladies and gentlemen, everything has a price! A beautiful home has a price. A successful marriage or relationship has a price. A wonderful friendship has a price. A college degree comes with a price. A great job has a price. The price is hard work, perseverance, and courage to take control of and change your destiny.

Be cautious when envying people that you perceive to be "successful." They have paid a price to be in that big house, drive that fancy car, or celebrate their 25th wedding anniversary. Remember, you can't tell what is going on inside of a house by looking at the outside. Appearances are deceiving. Your perception may not be reality. Instead of wishing you could be like them or have what they have, ask yourself if you are willing to pay what they paid. That question will always bring you back to earth.

Aspire to create your own "success" story. We all have one. We just need to take a moment to reflect on how far we have come. Remember how excited you were when you bought the house. Remember that you knew the house needed work. Remember that you were willing to accept the house as it was and work on the projects one at a time. You were willing to pay the price to get the house where you wanted it to be. So, when you reach an obstacle, revitalize your thought process. Resolve that you have the strength to endure this obstacle. Let your positive thoughts fuel your desire to survive. Remember that "**Everything Has A Price!**" Ask yourself, **are you willing to pay it?** Finally, understand that the same energy and strength you have used to survive gives you the power to succeed!

If you would like more information regarding
Veraunda Jackson speaking at your banquet, seminar,
workshop, university, company or any other event/venue:

Please contact her at:
Veraunda I. Jackson, Esquire
EHAP Inc.
P.O. Box 1150
Orlando, Florida 32802
407-445-1766 phone
407-445-0266 fax
or
send your inquiry via e-mail to:
ehapinc@aol.com

Visit Veraunda's website:
www.ehapinc.com

BOOK & TAPE
ORDER FORM

EHAP Inc.
Everything Has A Price!
P.O. Box 1150
Orlando, Florida 32802

407-445-1766 (p) or 407-445-0266 (f)
• Visit my website, www.ehapinc.com to order.
• Credit Card orders - fax or mail this order form
  for an autographed copy.

Name: _____

Address: _____

City, State, Zip: _____

Phone: _____

Name for Autograph: _____

Book: You Don't Have To Settle ____ x $18.00*= $ _____

Book: Everything Has A Price ____ x $18.00*= $ _____

Tape: Everything Has A Price ____ x $12.00*= $ _____

Tape: Legally Structuring Your Business ____ x $12.00*= $ _____

TOTAL = $ _____
*Includes shipping and handling

_____ I have enclosed a check or money order

_____ I am ordering by credit card

Credit Card Type *(Circle)*:   VISA   MC   AMEX

Number _____

Exp Date: _____ Total authorized: $ _____

Signature _____